LITTLE
SARA
OF
TEHRAN

A MEMOIR

SARA RAHIMI

Little Sara of Tehran

a memoir

By Sara Rahimi

Copyright © 2021 Sara Rahimi

All rights reserved. No part of this book may be reproduced or used in any manner without the prior written permission of the copyright owner,
except for the use of brief quotations in a book review.

To request permissions, contact the publisher at tabitha@lifetopaper.com

Paperback: 978-1-63760-202-7
Ebook: 978-1-63760-201-0

First paperback edition May 2021.

Edited by Jackie Brown and Tabitha Rose
Cover Design by Tabitha Rose and Arash Jahani
Front cover photo by Agnes Kiesz at Pure Studios
Back cover photo by: Arsia Soroushfar at Smart Shot
About the Author photograph: Azita Ziaei at Studiospec
Layout by Arash Jahani

Printed in the USA.

**Life to Paper Publishing Inc.
Toronto | Miami**

www.lifetopaper.com

To Anne,
Hope the story
inspire you :)
Sara
July 3,2024

Contents

Chapter One 12

Chapter Two 24

Chapter Three 38

Chapter Four 52

Chapter Five 64

Chapter Six 82

Chapter Seven 102

Chapter Eight 122

Chapter Nine 132

Chapter Ten 150

Chapter Eleven 160

Acknowledgements 172

About the Author 176

Disclaimer: This book is a memoir. It reflects the author's present recollections of experiences over time. Although some names have been changed, some events have been compressed, and some dialogue has been recreated, nothing has been invented or fabricated. Because this is a book of memory, and memory has its own story to tell, the author has done her best to make it a truthful story.

To my mother who gave me wings to fly.

&

To all women who want to break free from fear and live their truth.

Little Sara of Tehran

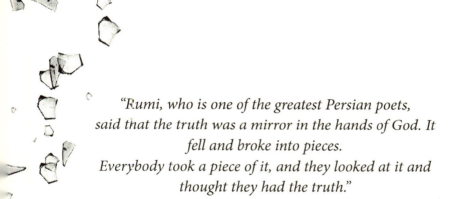

"Rumi, who is one of the greatest Persian poets, said that the truth was a mirror in the hands of God. It fell and broke into pieces. Everybody took a piece of it, and they looked at it and thought they had the truth."

~ Mohsen Makhmalbaf

Chapter One

"Your secret self is a true Wonder woman...so let her shine."

~ Lynda Carter

My heart is racing. We could be flogged, or even worse: forced to wed on the spot. He is not even my boyfriend— he is a family friend who came over to visit not knowing I was home alone. My sister and my mom are returning soon. There's nothing dirty happening here. I want to say this, but I cannot. I do not dare look into the eyes of the man yelling at us. Instead, I stare at his sandals. Both are caked in the dirt of the street. Coarse grey hairs spring from his toes. His toenails are gnarled and blackened. Omid, my friend, tries the front door of the apartment complex again. It still won't budge.

"I locked the front door and called the *Gasht-e Ershad*. You and your boyfriend are not going anywhere until you learn your lesson!"

I look up and see the smirk on the face of this man. He stares at me through narrowed eyes. My mouth is dry, and even if I could speak, I know there are no words that can calm him. We have done nothing but laugh, chat, and finish up our homework together. But it is against the rules to be with a boy. I am sixteen. I can think only of my dad and how if the police did come, all this would shame him and destroy my family. The man's small dark eyes are almost hidden by overgrown eyebrows, unruly hair grows all over his face.

Fear spreads in me like wildfire at his mention of the dreaded *Gasht-e Ershad*, the Morality Police. My teenage indignation rears up. This man, our neighbor, acts like he is the Islamic version of Superman, as though he's saving the country from the so-called moral defect that is supposedly spreading across the world because of people like me. His dirty feet in those ugly slippers make me want to throw up. But I cannot say a word and I dare not move. I am powerless. I grit my teeth. I must make sure my frustration does not show. I must try to look afraid— not defiant— or this will

Chapter One

get even worse.

I think of Baba, my father, "Don't you ever do anything to get caught or detained by the Morality Police. Don't shame me!" His voice is ringing in my ears. Then from my neighbor, "*Fased*!" The word slaps me, smothers me, covers me as if with tar.

I run upstairs and my friend follows. I cannot shame my father. I am his little princess. I had already disappointed him by failing algebra last year—during that bad time— in the middle of the worst of my parents' arguments. Now I wonder why I continue to push against the rules, as stupid as I think many of them are. This simple act of chatting with a boy could ruin my family. I could not face my parents if I were arrested and they had to bail me from some horrible place. My family's name would be in some government database. Bapa would be angry and disappointed. The rest of the family, too.

We rush inside the apartment and I slam the door. The threat of the Morality Police is clear, but it is the word he calls me that made me run. *Fased*. The strength of this shocking word— the judgement in his narrowed eyes, the possible punishment— pierce my soul. *Fased*. Little bitch. Corrupt. Bad girl. Whore. It is not safe. I bolt the locks and look around. Where? How can we hide?

"What should we do now?" Omid asks. "Maybe I should call my father?" He's terrified too.

My heart beats quickly, as if it's coming out of my chest. "No, we don't have time." I am listening for signs of anyone approaching, like feet marching up the cement stairs. It's evening and it is getting dark and cold outside.

Crying, I rush into my bedroom and grab the blue shawl that I wear in public as my hijab. I look outside my window. I open it and peer down to see how high above the ground we are.

"You must be kidding me!" Omid is shouting.

"I'd rather die than get caught by Morality Police. I'm sorry, but you have to jump." He looks at me in disbelief. "Come on!" I say. "We don't have time. You heard that old man. We have no other choice. He called the police. Grab the shawl and go. Now!"

He does. He jumps from the second-story window and breaks his arm. I never hear from him again.

***

Twenty years later and I am thirty-six, ready to jump again. This time from a plane, not a second-story window. I've made it to Canada. Again, my heart is racing, this time from excitement instead of fear. I am with Shawn, my male friend. We are adventurous and fun.

I've changed into a red jumpsuit with blue straps which, like most clothes made for adult women, is too big for me. I am worried, as I want the photos and the video— for which I have paid extra— to be perfect. As I walk out of the hangar toward the small aircraft, the camerawoman focusses the camera on my face.

"How are you feeling, Sara?" she asks.

"I'm thrilled and a bit scared. My adrenaline levels must be really, really high." I laugh.

"What made you decide to do this?"

I feel even more nervous now, as I try to look and sound good in front of the camera. I expected this question and have practiced an answer. I am aware that my English is accented. My Canadian friends, those who were born here, say I sound "charming." I doubt that. To my ears my English sounds clumsy and unrefined. My accent makes it clear that I am an outsider. I already struggle with the feeling I do not fit in and the way I speak English allows space for people to judge me. Today, I do not want to make any grammatical mistakes in my English or say anything that might ruin this experience for me. As extreme as this may seem, I have given this event a big job: jumping from this plane is my way of breaking from my past. So, I am smiling as I prepare to answer. I am always smiling; thus, no one seems to notice that I am nervous. I take a deep breath and reply, enunciating each carefully selected word: "I've always wanted to try skydiving. It's my birthday today, so I decided to face my fear and treat myself to this amazing gift."

"Well, good luck! See you up there!"

But behind the smile, I am still *Little Sara of Tehran,* hiding myself to maintain or gain the approval of my neighbors, my father, my uncles, or my (now ex) husband and his family: all of them are part of the life I had back in Iran. Even here, thousands of miles away, I hear their voices in my head telling me that I am ridiculous for wanting what I want, and immoral for not doing things their way. Yet, I refuse to let my fear of not being who they want me to be stop me any longer. To them it is unfathomable that I choose to live far from home, on my own, when I could be living in comfort and luxury as the trophy wife of an ambitious city lawyer. They were shocked by every decision I made that took me further away from their ideas of "the social norm." To them I am crazy for abandoning all that they consider to be the best things in life. And as hard as I try, as I do Canadian things, like try on a revealing, sexy dress, I am reminded of the familiar judgement always in the air in Iran. As I look at myself in the mirror, I cannot prevent myself from imagining what they would say. I hear their voices say, "that's too short" and I see their faces staring back at me with disgust and impatience. *Why do you keep pushing the rules?* I imagine them saying. I shudder as I feel my ex-husband's dismissal of me. I can all but hear his eyes roll as he says with that condescending tone, *why bother your pretty head with that,* as I try to concentrate on writing a book or running my business.

Their verbal judgement kept me hostage for too long. Now, I need to stop letting my fear of their disapproval keep me bound when they are thousands and thousands of miles away. But I am surprised by how they still enslave me. My past life affects my perception of myself despite the self-improvement work I am doing, and like the way tiny grains of sand can ease their way between large stones in a jar, the negative thoughts push their way into all crevices of my mind. I tell myself that I am jumping from a plane to be free: to break the chains of shame and unworthiness that have held me back. The fear of their judgement is still stronger than the fear of any parachuting mishap. I figure if I can skydive— the one thing that terrifies me the most— I can conquer the world. I can conquer anything. I can conquer me.

The wind blows my short hair as I climb the stairs into the plane and soon, we are soaring higher and higher. Below me, I see the flat area where spectators are waiting for their loved ones to land. I look at the other three risk takers who are geared up and attached to their instructors, just as I am. I wonder if they also have butterflies in their stomachs. I defuse my nervousness by making funny faces and joking with Shawn and my instructor. I need to look strong for the camera that is still running, after all.

As the plane continues to rise higher in the sky, all I see is clouds. My mouth is dry and internally, I can hear each of my heartbeats. But I still keep up the smile. Externally, the drone of the aircraft drowns out most of the jokes I try to yell to Shawn. I almost pee my pants when the instructor announces it's time to jump. One instructor opens the blinds. Seriously, the opening cannot be called a door. It rolls up like blinds on the windows I have at home. She motions for us to come. I do. I am at the door and I look down. It's too windy and too high up.

"Are you ready, Sara?" my instructor asks, her mouth just above my ear. We are strapped together.

No, I'm not! I say to myself. "Yes" I say aloud. I hold on to the top bar tightly, as if my life depends on it.

"One…. two…" she is counting, and my smile disappears as I try to remember what position I need to be in. She peels my hand off the top bar and by "three," we are in the air. We free fall at one hundred and twenty miles per hour for thirty seconds. As I hurtle downwards, the force of the wind stretches my face in all kinds of angles. I wave at the camera, but I make sure not to move too much.

"This is so freaking exciting!" I shout from the bottom of my lungs to make sure my voice is heard and recorded above the racket of the wind.

She pulls the ripcord, the parachute opens, and we get sucked back upwards. We are no longer rushing towards the ground. Our descent has slowed, and I can enjoy the views around me. I am struck by the beauty of Lake Ontario and the dramatic skyline of Toronto. From up here, there is beauty in the long and winding path of the traffic-jam prone highway and its miniature cars below. It looks perfect and orderly from this high above. I feel free and at peace: strong like an eagle. Unstoppable. As we land, I am certain that nothing can prevent me from living my life in a way that's true to me. This was the greatest birthday gift I've ever given myself. I need this feeling to last…

I had no doubts about my place as a second-class citizen in

Iran; I relied on female cajoling and manipulation to get what I wanted in the chauvinistic land of my birth. I knew how far I could get despite the often-turbulent political situation. My parents grew up during the time of the Shah, when the country was governed by a monarchy. At the time the economy was booming due to oil and the ruling Shah's attitudes were not dissimilar to leaders in Western countries; religion and politics were not entwined. Some in Iran were upset by the family's lavish lifestyle and did not want Western values to influence the nation. The Islamic Revolution of 1979 brought a change. The Shah and many of those who supported him were banished from Iran or wisely left the country. The new government encouraged people to maintain strictly enforced Islamic rules.

But I was around three or four when the change in government was happening. I grew up in a loving family and it wasn't until I was a teenager that I saw how the religious-based rules would restrict and limit my opportunities simply because I was female. And the rules extended outside of Iran, too. Most countries would not let us freely enter like they did before the revolution. We need to have VISAs to travel, plus our previously buoyant economy was squashed despite the oil. Our currency remains devalued.

Yet it was still my home. I knew what to do, where to go, and how to act. I knew to be fearful of any white SUVs with *Gasht-e Ershad* stamped in green. I knew all the unwritten rules: what was considered cool, what clothing and jewelry would indicate high social status within the community, and what to hide about myself. I understood when to pay taxes, what to do if I needed medical treatment, as well as where in Tehran's markets I could go to find the freshest lemons. I was a daughter, and by the time I was twenty-five, I was also a wife. I knew my role in society, in my family, and in my marriage. I was born into the language and absorbed its rules. The rules, all of them, became mine.

Chapter One

But here in Canada, having achieved the goal of citizenship, I felt unsure. I still had a lump in my throat at times. I carried a nagging feeling that I was missing some small but important thing, like understanding what x was in a mathematical equation. I feared that I would never belong here and live without question of my place in society. There were so many obvious reasons to leave Iran, but I was traumatized by my past and could not settle. I think many immigrants feel the same way and this can be heightened for women who grew up in a culture which oppressed them and made them feel vulnerable to sudden repercussions, even from strangers on the street. I felt too visible and because of the ever-present self-doubt, I felt broken by my well-hidden lack of confidence. The fear that I was going to misunderstand people, due to some nuance of Canadian culture and language, and make an embarrassing mistake was always there.

I was grateful that day, as I stood ready for the camera and I wanted to rid myself of the feeling that this was a mixed blessing. I had made it to Toronto, my teenage dream, but I was on my own; that was not how it was supposed to be. My husband promised to join me, but he did not. There was always some excuse for his absence. Despite my ability to forgive his crushing betrayal of our marriage vows, he nonetheless abandoned me here without the status of wife. I had far less money than I was used to, and I was adjusting to depending on public transportation after having to sell our BMW. That and the condo, which I was also considering selling, were intended for our new life here together.

I decided to divorce him against his wishes and despite the criticism of the uncles who remained a big part of my life. Although I was fairly sure that divorce was the right choice, I still second-guessed nearly every decision that I made. I was rattled by the challenges of settling down and starting from scratch. The nightly calls with my mother helped. She encouraged me to stay in Canada and live the dream I had since my teenage years. But a few short months after my arrival in Canada, she died. Suddenly. With no hint of illness—none that she admitted to me, anyway. The loneliness of losing my mother and being far away from my sister—physically as well emotionally— haunted me. I fought hard to belong, nevertheless, I never felt as comfortable in my own skin here as I did in Iran. Deep down, I will always be a Persian woman. Could I really become a Canadian one, too?

As a young woman in Iran, I used to watch Oprah on satellite TV although non-Iranian channels were banned at the time. I would think how interesting it was that women were brave enough to go on the show and share intimate details about their lives, how courageously they chose to take a different path. I admired them. I admired *Oprah* and *Ellen* and their guests who were often women who did not follow the life expected of them, where they filled the role of the obedient wife or where they chose an ordinary career. Instead, they followed their instincts with brave independence. I admired the ones who chose to overcome a victim mentality by speaking their truths and thus taking control of their destinies. I admired the women who had enough respect for themselves and valued their worth. The ones who were unwilling to take any crap from anyone.

As I watched them on television in Iran, I wanted to be one of them. I wanted to learn more, see more, do more, and be more. I wanted to be my own superhero. Jumping out of a plane, I thought, will help me do this. This act of undeniable bravery would be the symbol that I needed to prove to myself that this woman, Little Sara of Tehran and now of Canada, would let no boundary whether internal or external prevent her from becoming all she wanted to be.

Looking back at the films of that day now, I think of that

Chapter One

thirty-six-year-old Sara as naïve. Little did that version of me know that my fears were so deeply embedded into my being that I would need far more than possibly falling to my death to help me step into my greatness. I needed to learn how to be a divorced Persian woman in a bustling, unfriendly city in a new country where I did not know anyone. I needed to learn how to overcome my fears of disapproval and failure, while contending with my fear of telling my story. I publish this book knowing that this act of bravery may bring judgement and ridicule from friends and family, perhaps even repercussions and persecution of loved ones I left behind. But I must move forward and that is why I have written this book: my story. I know I am not alone in the difficulty of creating a new life in a strange new land. I hope this helps many women remove the mask and live authentically and free, as I do now.

Chapter Two

"We are born of love. Love is our mother."

~ *Rumi*

Little Sara of Tehran

I was born in the right place: Tehran, the capital city of Iran, in the Middle East. We are loud and expressive yet have much in common with the British "stiff upper lip" culture. Every emotion is expressed in our words, our body language, our food. Thus, the fact that I was born a crier and a screamer did not alarm my poor mother. I let her know I was uncomfortable through my temper tantrums. Even now, one of the things that connects me to my Greek-Canadian fiancé is his complete understanding and acceptance of how I can dissolve into tears when strong emotions—sadness, fear, or joy—overtake me.

Could my fiery personality be due to the warmth of the air in my homeland, the breezes that smell of the sea and spices, and the saffron in Persian food? Iranians are loud; within a family setting or at a party we ensure everyone knows what we want and desire, but it is all said in a subtle way. Afterall, we are careful, especially us women, to avoid upsetting anyone. Our outspokenness at home only comes when gossiping about others; we judge and condemn our neighbors with great vigor. However, never to their face!

Maybe it is because it is the norm to live in close physical proximity with extended family that we do not demand the personal space that requires bottling things up. Iranian homes are always full of people and when they visit, they are encouraged to stay. With the placement of a cloth or rugs, a room changes purpose. The dining room becomes a bedroom and us kids share the space fully with our parents, aunts, cousins, and grandparents. My grandparents' home was usually full of visitors.

It was on the weekends that our whole family got together. We visited my mother's family, and I could not wait to get spoiled by my six uncles. My unmarried uncles were still living at home. My married uncles and their wives were already there when we arrived. Sayeh, my elder sister, and I were the first-born grandkids.

Chapter Two

We were showered with love. But there were always fights between Sayeh and our youngest uncle, Shahin. His nickname was *shah pesar* meaning "king boy." Shahin was my grandmother's favorite, and we all knew it and I was the spoiled baby.

It was a simple two-story house with a stone-tiled front yard. Decorative plants in pots lined the path to the door. The smell of jasmine welcomed guests. Even today, the smell of jasmine instantly takes me back to my grandparent's home. In the center of the yard was a water fountain. I greeted the goldfish who lived in it before going into the house. I would go inside just long enough to say hello to my grandparents and uncles, then I would escape back out to the front yard. My job was to water the flowers and the many pots that surrounded the fountain and pathway. I spent a long time doing this, because I also talked to each plant and watered the ants.

My grandmother had to come out to check on me as I spent considerable time on this favorite chore. "Sara, what are you doing?" my grandmother asked, with a big smile on her face. "Now I'm watering the ants, Maman Mehri. They're thirsty."

The aroma of my grandmother's cooking often drew me inside. I would put away the hose and run in, hopeful that everything was ready so I would not have to smell great food without being able to taste it. Grandma made the best *sabzi polo*, rice with fresh dill, cilantro, and parsley. We ate it with fried fish. Everyone helped to set the dining table, but most often we spread a big tablecloth on the floor and sat around it to eat. Persian carpets were multi-layered on all the surfaces, hung on walls and piled on the floor. Sitting on the floor was comfortable. We had cushions for the older relatives. In the spring—when the weather was beautiful and the flowers were in bloom— we took the cloth, carpets, and pillows, and set them up in the yard, like a picnic.

There was always plenty of food with new servings coming

out, one after another. Yogurt and fine herbs, like parsley, basil, mint, and thinly chopped leek were there in abundance. And afterward, cleaning up and washing the dishes was easy. It was a family matter, and everyone helped. One person soaped and then passed the dish to the next person who rinsed, passing to the next person who dried. My grandmother put the dishes away. As I grew older and less clumsy, it was an honor that she allowed me to help her do that.

My uncles got into their pajamas after lunch and laid down on the floor to watch TV while the women served tea and sweets. "Sara, *daei*, can you walk on my back?" Uncle Shahin asked. He'd turn to lie on his stomach and say, "keep walking, Sara" then "good, Sara, keep walking right there!" I loved walking on my uncles' backs. They got their massages and I got to practice my balance. I had the balance and stature of a gymnast. By the time I was seven, I imagined myself in the Olympics, with many heavy gold medals hanging from my neck.

My grandfather knew the poems of great poets like Hafez, Saadi, and Molana by heart. In his later years, when I knew him, Grandfather never spoke his mind directly. He always gave lessons or expressed his opinion through poetry. Once, when my sister and I were arguing, grandfather said, "Raise your words, not voice. It is rain that grows flowers, not thunder." We both stopped what we were doing to look at him. There was nothing to say. Neither of us understood what he meant, but we knew he was wise and felt that he'd blessed us somehow. Quoting Rumi turned out to be a much stronger way of gaining peace than yelling, "shut up!" It certainly stopped that argument.

Eating fruit after lunch or after a short nap was a must. Apples, oranges, pears, plums, watermelon, and grapes were shared on large ceramic dishes. The fruit served depended on the season, but there were always big plates passed around, overflowing with fruits. My favorite was juicy pomegranate. My uncles removed the seeds and gathered them in a bowl for me.

After a full lunch we occasionally headed out for a walk. We were always fifteen minutes from nature. Tehran is a densely populated city surrounded by two beautiful mountain ranges. We walked to the park or—my favorite—went hiking in Darband. Darband was a popular local spot for families: its trails swirl up to the top of Mount Tochal.

The foot of the mountain was crowded with young people, couples, and families starting and ending their hikes. Vendors sold everything from fruit, flowers, spices, snacks, and toys. There were so many colourful things to see there.

"No, no let's stay away from the market!" my mother said, pulling me away from the vendors and toward the hiking trails. "I don't want to have Sara crying for something today."

The steep hike to the top of the mountain took a few hours, so it was a treat when we journeyed the whole way. When I got tired, my uncles took turns carrying me on their shoulders. From there, I could see best. I could see all the small cafes and vendors. I craved and called out for a chance to taste the yummy fruit pastes and other munchies, but these requests were often ignored. I wondered if it was because I was so high up that they could not hear me.

As we hiked higher and higher up the mountain, the sounds of chatter around cafes disappeared to be replaced by the sound of the river crashing downwards. In some places, there was no handrail or fence on the outside edge of the trail. Still, families would climb and jostle each other as they went up and down the stony steps that were conveniently carved into the trail.

"Let me carry her now," Uncle Hamid said to Uncle Shahin

as we set off up the mountain again. "*Baba jan*, put her down to walk, she's a strong girl. Aren't you, Sara?" Uncle Sohrab said, and I got down. I did not want to, but I wanted to prove that I was indeed strong. However, when we got to the top of the mountain, I demanded to be lifted again. From the top, we could see the entire city beneath us. At night, we could see the lights of all the homes, the bustling of the cafes, and the cars moving, tiny, like beetles below.

At times, my dad filmed us with his Super Eight camera. He liked capturing moments from our family adventures. He was in the movie industry and owned one of the main movie theatres just three hours outside of Tehran. It was such an important feature of the city that it was purposely burned down during the Islamic Revolution, perhaps because they also played some Hollywood movies. These movies were seen as anti-Islamic by the new rulers who favored a more conservative view of family, and women in particular. But Baba rebuilt it. He was very proud of the work he did. People flock to his theatre to watch government-approved American movies. In my father's studio, the voice-over actors dubbed the English dialogue into Persian for Iran's movie-goers.

My mother studied acting and had a beautiful voice. She worked as a film dubber, acting out the parts of famous Hollywood actors, like Yvette Mimieus in *Where the Boys Are*, translated into Farsi. It is through movie work that my parents met, my father hired her. But once my parents got married, my father did not allow her to continue her work as an actress, or in any other job, despite my mother's desire to have a career. This caused many problems in their marriage.

I loved my mother and I loved being with my mother. However, when I was young, I wondered why she was never concerned about things I knew other moms would worry about. I wondered why she was always so relaxed about things. I will never forget the scariest movie I ever watched. I was seven or eight when movie night featured *The Exorcist*. I was squeezed between my uncles with a big pillow on my lap, ready to cover my face in order to avoid the scariest of the horror scenes. I screamed and buried my face in the pillow as the girlish voice of the twelve-year-old main character transformed into a devilish deep man's growl. I peeked out from the pillow and saw her fly up above her bed, hovering, with the unwavering priest holding up a cross in an attempt to get the devil out of her body. My uncles hugged me, but they also laughed and teased me, making the voice themselves over the following weekends just to see my reactions and hear me scream.

"Mom! Why would you let me watch such a movie?" I asked her.

"That's just a movie, it's not real! And I know, even if I warned you, you would want to watch it anyway. Besides, you were surrounded by your strong uncles. Nothing is going to happen to you with them around." She smiled and patted me on the head.

Later, when I thought back about incidents like that, I realized that she always treated me like I had intelligence. She wasn't one to baby kids. Thus, I grew up with the sense that she trusted and believed in me so much that she knew I could handle things. This made me believe in myself, even in the times when this tiny flame was almost extinguished by shame and fear. She was never overprotective, and I believe that is part of what allowed me to handle the many traumas I was to survive in the future.

The first real memory I have of my mother starts with me bawling my eyes out while in her arms. I was around three. Maman had already dropped off my sister, Sayeh, to school. As Sayeh stood waving good-bye to us, I thought that she looked like a big girl. There she was in her school uniform: a grey long jacket with matching grey pants. Part of the uniform was a white *maghnaeh*, a type of cotton head covering that looks similar to the head coverings worn by Catholic nuns. Sayeh waved then turned around to run off to her classroom, disappearing into a sea of grey and white. It was then that I started to snivel. I knew what was coming. Maman would take me to daycare and leave me too.

By the time Maman pulled away from my sister's school, I was crying so intensely that I could hardly breathe. We arrived at the daycare and I saw smiling bunnies, *Tom and Jerry,* as well as *Mickey Mouse* on the walls. But that was not enough to console me. Maman said something to me, but I could not respond. She opened the car door and leaned in to pick me up into her arms. Although my family called me Little Sara because I was smaller than most kids my age, when I was upset, I was as strong as those three times my size. I squirmed to avoid her arms, then braced my body, as rigid as a plank of wood. Beautiful Maman smelled nice and was dressed, as usual, in a black *manto,* an elegant type of cloak, along with a colorful scarf that showed only half of her beautiful black hair. The other mothers led their nice, calm children to the door of the building. They were dressed similarly. I didn't even register that the children, the parents, and the teachers stared at me as I screamed and struggled against my mother.

Maman brushed her mouth against my ear. "Elahi ghorboonet beram. Geryeh nakon," she whispered. *I love you, don't cry,* my mother soothes although the exact translation of the first phrase is "I would destroy myself for you" a curious way that Iranians express their love for each other. But I could not stop the tornado of torment in my little body. She was going to leave me. Just then, I felt her turn around and carry me back to the parked car. She put me in my seat, and we drove off.

I continued to cry and was surprised to see that Maman had

stopped in front of a giant store with a huge window. All I saw were toys. Colorful ones. We rush in and Maman goes straight to the aisle with the musical instruments. I stopped crying and looked around. My face lit up when I saw a perfect little guitar. It was red, yellow, orange, and blue. It was almost my size.

Maman held me. She handed me the guitar and I lifted it as I bumped up and down in her arms. Maman was rushing. She paid in cash and was called back for her change. We rushed back to the car and within minutes, we were back at my daycare. Maman walked me to class and waited for me behind the window. I entered happily and showed-off my colorful new guitar.

But the morning was not always as hectic as that one. If he was in the city, my dad woke me up. "Pasho dokhtar e golam," he'd say while brushing my bushy eyebrows with his finger. *Get up, my beautiful girl!*. Later, when I am around thirteen, after he strokes my eyebrows, he adds, "Don't you ever pluck these beautiful eyebrows, leave them as they are. Natural."

"Yeah" I would reply. "I'll leave them as *pache boz,* so I look like a goat, Dad. Great advice. That way no boy will look at me."

Breakfast is always brewed tea with sugar, *barbari* or *sangak*— types of whole wheat leavened flatbread—with walnuts and *lighvan paneer,* feta cheese. Sometimes we have eggs. Bread and cheese are my favorite. I would eat them at all meals if I could, not just breakfast! That's how I earned my second nickname: *Sara Noon Paneeri*—Sara Bread and Cheesy.

My parents take turns driving us to school or we take Service. Service is a minivan that picks up a few kids in the neighborhood and drives them to school. Because I've always been smaller than children my age, I am made to sit at the front row or stand at the front of the line at the school yard. In the morning, we line up with our class and listen to announcements. We stretch and then sing several songs including the national anthem.

Since God has blessed me with a strong voice, I am the solo singer at the school choir each year. I love it. Being in the spotlight feels good. The songs I am asked to sing are national anthems or rousing revolutionary songs. I sing them so passionately that I feel like a warrior. After school, Sayeh and I have extra classes to attend. We go to English classes, gymnastics, ice-skating, and piano lessons.

I do not like piano lessons nor the cats that my teacher lets roam all over her place, but I do like her library and study room. My sensitivity to being scolded frustrates her. Even then I feared being judged, and her pointing out my errors was too much for me. "Oh my God, Mrs. Rahimi! Get a jar to collect your daughter's tears. Why does she cry every time I mention she plays a wrong note?"

By the time we get home, I am starving and the smell of freshly steamed rice with saffron and some type of stew or *khoresh*, makes me feel faint. We sit together at the table—my mother, my sister, my father, and I—to eat and talk about our days at school. Afterward, my sister and I are allowed to watch cartoons for a short time until it is time for homework.

I am ten or eleven years old when homework becomes serious business. If either my sister or I were to receive a grade as low as an A- on our report cards, we have to see a tutor to make sure we bring up our marks back to the A+ level. No other grade is acceptable in my home. I find this difficult, but my sister does not. She is far more studious than I. It is like she chews every bit of information from books like a mouse. She is always ready for her many exams. I am the sporty one who loves gymnastics. I also write poetry. I can see that I take academics less seriously than she does. For her, things are right or wrong; I am more comfortable with grey zones.

While trying to study, I can almost feel when it is approaching 6 o'clock in the evening. My body is restless. I am waiting to hear my mom's loud voice tremble through the walls: "Sayeh! Sara! *Ab porteghal hazere!*" We were spoiled, my sister and I. Maman is calling us to come grab freshly squeezed orange juice. I sip my juice slowly. I am in no rush to get back to my books.

At this time of the evening, I notice how tired Maman is. From preparing meals, to cleaning the home, taking us to five different classes, to hosting parties, she was also doing things for us or for my father. Maybe this is why she infused us with independence, telling us not to get married young despite the fact that many girls around us tended to do just that. From the time I was a young girl, I remember my mother telling my sister to "meet and date a few men, travel, work, and make money. Then get married." By the time my sister is a teenager, she is head-strong and rebellious. Me, a little less so. Maman is doing all she can to keep the relationship between my sister and I and our father civil. "Stop putting me between you and your dad. I'm so tired of covering up for you girls," Maman said every time she had to lie about where we were or why we returned home late. But it did not seem as though there was much that she could do to keep her own relationship with our father peaceful. They were often arguing.

"You didn't let me work! All these years!" She cries as she yells this. "I would have been independent like all the other dubbers. I would have much more. A better life!"

"You are in a much better place financially than those women!" my dad spits back. "How can you not see what I've provided for you?"

Their fights scare me. They erupt most days without warning, but often start in the latter half of the evening. I try to be invisible and slink out of the room. I run off to study. However, in my bedroom, I still hear them. I see the scene as if it was played out in front of me: the redness and the veins popping on my father's face, the fury in his eyes, my mother wailing with her head down on the table. Then Baba looks at her, shaking his head. "You don't appreciate what I have done in life." From upstairs for a while, all I hear is Maman's crying. Eventually, I hear the door slam and go out to see her. Watching him leave makes her angrier, and she cries and cries.

For me, the sound of the door slam is a big relief. At least with Baba gone, the argument is over. I can try to calm her down although I do not understand exactly what it is that bothers her. Their arguments terrify me, and the continuing pattern of their unhappiness confuses me. Our lives seem like the lives of my friends' parents. Their mothers do not work either. I am too afraid to ask any of my friends if their mothers are as unhappy as mine. I know my family dynamic is not normal.

As I rub her back and bring her a glass of water, I wonder what the big deal is. We have everything we need. Don't we?

Chapter Three

*"People will forget what you said.
People will forget what you did.*

*But people will never forget how
you made them feel."*

~ Maya Angelou

"Your mom was such a brave and daring woman. If she had the support of her family, she would've achieved way more in her life." My heart breaks when Uncle Mehrad tells me this, even though I already knew this to be true.

We go through the family photographs he has brought with him. I have been looking forward to this visit—he comes with his wife, Maha, who is my favorite. I have been in Canada for ten years and this is my opportunity to show off my new homeland. It is the summer I am writing this book. I still have many unanswered questions about my mother and for the first time, I start asking them.

"No, she didn't get any support," he says. "And that's a pity."

I look at him in disgust, tears roll down my face. "Just like the time I was getting divorced and none of you supported me."

He nods, looking past me, as if into nothingness. He knows they had not supported either of us. He continues talking. "Your grandfather, our father, made her marry when she was thirteen. Her first husband was a cousin and much older. I remember the arguments although I don't remember him clearly. It was so long ago. Your mother was thirteen and I was younger. She wasn't happy about it, but she could not get our father to change his decision on it. She was to marry him and that was it. That's how things worked back then. In a traditional home, a girl would get her first period at her husband's house. Girls used to marry young, Sara. Grandfather mellowed in his old age, but back then he was loud and strict. And you know your mother. She always spoke her mind. But she could not fight this. She was made to marry and to leave home."

After a few glasses of wine, my aunt and I begin singing the songs my mother used to sing while my uncle drinks beer. After each beer, he cries. He shakes his head as he remembers something

Chapter Three

important about his sister—my mother—a beautiful and vibrant woman who died too young.

My mom was called Safieh. She was both the only and eldest daughter of seven children. Her six loving younger brothers protected her and nicknamed her *Paloon do kaleh*, a silly joke that implied she had enough hair for two heads. She was beautiful and wore her long, thick black hair in one braid as a child. When she grew up, it was always worn in a beautiful updo.

Her parents were religious and strict. She went to school but was not expected to do much outside of her home as an adult. Her own mother, my beloved Maman Mehri, could not read or write, and lived this traditional life. So, although Maman Mehri may not have agreed with it, but she did not prevent the marriage of her young daughter. As a woman, her place was to go along with the wishes of her husband and to support cultural expectations. However, after a few months of marriage, my mother was still very unhappy. Maman Mehri saw the effects of her child being forced into adulthood and she would not remain silent. She helped my mother get out of that marital home and eventually, after four years, obtain a divorce. Despite tradition, my grandmother pushed against the rules to save her daughter.

According to my uncle, once back at home, all my mother wanted was to go back to school but she was now behind her peers. Maman Mehri sent my mom to night school to catch up with the rest of her classmates. She ordered Mehrad to go with my mom. "Safieh is not to walk alone at night," she told her son.

My mother was intelligent and studious, and it was no surprise she maintained excellent grades and was accepted into the best university in Iran, the University of Tehran. Women were expected to study to become teachers and nurses; despite her parents' objection, my mother studied drama and got her Bachelor of Arts. My grandfather was religious, and it was believed that the arts, particularly drama and music were not appropriate for women. To men like him, seeing their daughters acting or singing in public would be like burning in hell's fires while still alive! Yet she persisted. While she was studying, she was also hosting a radio channel. She had a great voice. My mother was an exceptional woman.

After university, Safieh acted in a few plays at the theatre. She loved it. She made good money and she was even helping my grandparents pay off their mortgage. She was a young girl and a divorcee with six brothers, far more independent than most women were allowed to be during that time, but she still did not have full freedom. She was regularly criticized for what she wore. She was a stylish young woman, gorgeous and chic, who continuously flouted the rules of traditional Islamic fashions by preferring western clothing.

"No miniskirts allowed! You are showing too much skin," my grandfather told her, but she ignored his judgement. She took off, heading to her job, and later, went out to enjoy herself and meet with friends. She met my father when she was dubbing at my father's studio. She got to voicet the parts of the American classic girl with the right levels of intensity and emotion for the large audience of Persian film goers. She married her boss (my father) after a year of dating.

It is a wonder she was able to date him that long, considering her parents were traditional and strict. Plus, she had six brothers who, despite being younger than her, learned they could impose their views on her way of life. Her job meant she saw and acted in modern films, her Western fashion was not modest, and she was spending time with a man who was not yet her husband: none of this was acceptable to her father but in Tehran, the styles on the street were similar to those in London, Paris, and New York. My grandfather was probably very relieved when their engagement was cemented through marriage. Perhaps because she was a divorcee and the family wanted to keep it quiet, there was no wedding. I'm not sure. As a child, I often wondered why there were no wedding pictures. Then I discovered my Maman had been married before.

"She was quite a rebel," Uncle Mehrad stated. "Always trying to do things her way, but mostly she couldn't because it was not allowed. That's the way it was," he insisted when he saw my face. He huffed, and stood to get up, bumping the table in his haste to get away. I fumed; my heartbroken for my mother. My eyes bore holes in his back. I watched as he squeezed lemons in the salad his wife had prepared. I teased him. In a sing-song voice I praised the "enormous" efforts he was making towards the evening meal. I see his shoulders shake with rage. "You are a feminist, just like her," he said, his face reddening due to his own upset and the alcohol.

I knew that ignoring their criticisms and standing up to them must have been difficult for my mother. I had faced them myself. The energy drained out of me, and I had nothing more to say. It was late. No need to provoke any further outbursts from Mehrad. The next day, I kept things light. I made sure we had a fun day at Niagara Falls, eating junk food, picking up shabby touristy gifts, and walking in the warmth and sunshine. I was so happy to have family with me.

"Your father was religious," he said that evening as we were enjoying the *fesenjoon* stew that his wife had made. I put my fork down and sighed. My eyes opened wide.

"Excuse me? 'Religious'? Who would marry a divorcee? We're talking fifty-five years ago, for God's sake!" I was trying to hide my irritation because this visit taught me how little my uncle understood people. "I am not sure that my father even believed in God. But I'll never forget how he would kiss Maman's forehead when she said her prayers although he never said any himself. But he was strict and prejudiced, just like so many Persian men."

I thought about how the fact that my father forbade my mom from working always came up in my parents' fights. Just as her parents had clipped Maman's wings by forcing her to marry so young. Her husband—my father—clipped her wings too. He believed that acting, dubbing, and any other role in the film industry was not appropriate for women. That's why he never really let Sayeh and I even watch the dubbers doing the voice overs. He did not want us in that environment. He even protested when Maman bought the piano and put us through piano lessons, saying, "You want to raise our daughters as *motreb*." He felt playing the piano was not good for his daughters, associating music with "cheap, low-classed entertainers," as opposed to academics which would lead them to becoming doctors and respectability.

But that creative environment was what my mother craved. She was not born to live a life without art and curiosity, which was the traditional role of the Iranian housewife. She was way more independent-minded than that. She was like an eagle in a cage, flapping and breaking its wings due to its confining borders. She wanted to learn more, see more, do more, and be more. She needed a life where she could contribute to society through working, through helping others. As a result, my parents always fought as his word was the law due to the fact that women had little legal standing in Iran. As a housewife, her job was to take care of my father and bless the union and both of their families by having his babies. However, my mother was not interested in having children. She had Sayeh and I because my father and society insisted. He loved kids. Although she had not, at first, wanted to start a family, she was a loving and devoted mother to us both.

Chapter Three

"You didn't let me work. I could've been highly successful like the other women!" she said. I will forever hear the way Maman cried and screamed during their frequent arguments.

"You would've had less than we have now if you were working as a dubber. You have lived a better life!" my father yelled back, as if that was worth my mother's frustrations.

For my mother, it was not about having a bigger house, it was about having a meaningful life. My mom continued to study. She explored psychology and took classes on personal growth. She read many self-help books and had a large library. She found joy in leading large groups through all that she learned. She took my sister and I with her to her workshops.

I was curious and liked to go because there were always plenty of snacks. The school that mother attended was called Pana. The word and the theme of the movement can be translated as "nurturing human power or forces." It was founded by Dr. Ebrahim Khajeh Noori. He was a highly educated man: a psychologist, who practiced law and published many journalistic articles. He introduced the work of prominent psycho-analysts, such as Sigmund Freud and Karen Horney, to Iranians. Dr. Khajeh Noori trained a few devotees, like my mom, to host School of Pana classes. These students were teaching life skills way back in the eighties. What seems so modern now, what we call "coaching" today, was being taught in living rooms in Iran so many decades ago. I remember the psycho-drama roleplays as they seemed such fun and I had never seen adults "playing" like that.

The meeting locations rotated, taking place at a different member's house each time. Thirty or more members gathered together to discuss how to communicate effectively, how to look at the positive side of things, how to keep peace, and how to practice kindness. Maman was not getting paid for this work, but she loved it and there was a buzz of excitement at the meetings. Maman is very smart and is good at this, I remember thinking to myself. How can she lead a big group of people like this? I was proud of her. My father was less impressed. "You are *khodshifteh*." Narcissistic. "You like all the attention you get from those people around you." Then, he impersonated a supposed attendee, speaking in falsetto: "'Today I stepped off a curb and I didn't kill an ant' and the rest of you clap and cheer her."

But some of my mother's acts of self-determination were potentially dangerous in a country like Iran. Morality Police are not just men, as people in the West may think based on the sexism inherent in many Islamic countries. Women can be quite powerful civilian enforcers of the rules and thus women known as *Gasht e ershad* Sisters, fully covered in black chadors, hunt in pairs, watching women as they move about the city, ready to pounce at any sign of deviance from Islamic rules. They drag women to waiting Morality Police SUVs. When one such woman touched my mother, when we were shopping, Maman told her to take her hands off her. "Don't you touch me. You have no right to touch me or to take me anywhere."

The problem is the Morality Sisters, partners of the Morality Police, did indeed have these rights. They can do anything. On this day, they dragged us, my mom and twelve-year-old me, to the station where my mother was charged some kind of hijab or clothing infraction. She was made to sign a paper vowing she would not break the rules again and then allowed to call my father who collected us and took us home. Of course, this sparked another fight between them. "Why did you fight them?" my father asked. The fact that she did not go willingly to the station was mentioned on the form. "Why not just go with them? Where does this fighting get you?" he asked.

Chapter Three

Their arguments got worse once she got more deeply involved in the self-help movement. My mom was growing while my father remained the same person. My mother could not tolerate the difference between them anymore. When I was thirteen, she left him, moved out of the house, and they divorced. She was tired of the fighting, she said. She moved back in with her family and left my sister and I with our father. Living with her own parents was the only way to do it back then. I knew that. A divorced or single woman was not socially accepted. There was nowhere else for my mother to go.

Meanwhile, my father's sister, Pari, who lived in Denmark separated from her husband and moved back to Tehran. My father invited her to come live at our house to take care of Sayeh and I. What a disaster! We did not want her at our home. We wanted our mother. Our father thought he was helping Aunt Pari by having her stay with us. In return, she helped him by cooking and cleaning.

I hated those days! Although I did not want to live with my aunt, I had to respect her, nonetheless. My sister and I visited our mom as often as we could. It was strange and sad. "She has no other place to go," my father said when I complained about Aunt Pari. "Yes, she does! She has adult kids here as well as her sister," I reminded him, but he would not budge.

Sayeh and I argued with her. We were bitter and had a "you can't replace my mom" type of attitude. We had not seen our aunt in years and now she was bossing us around. How on Earth did she think she could pop into our lives at this difficult time and think she was doing us a favor? we thought. When my mother saw her at the house, she argued with her too.

"You think you are the new mother or something? Go and leave my daughters alone!"

But my aunt had no plans to leave. She felt needed.

To my school friends, it must have seemed like my mother had vanished. I could not let anyone at school know my parents had divorced. It was taboo. There was not a single example that I knew of where other children were living with one parent unless the other parent had died. A divorce was not anything I had expected, despite how unhappy they were as a couple. I did not know how to deal with the situation. I was thirteen, the age of my mother when she was married off. I felt lost and alone, like she had at my age. It was one more thing I did not know how to fix.

It was no easier for my mother to live with her parents and be around her own family. My uncles badgered her about leaving her husband and about leaving us. They constantly pushed for her to go back to him. My father avoided the whole situation by having his sister replace his wife. He tried to pretend nothing had changed when everything had, in fact, changed in our lives.

One day, three of my uncles arrive at our home. They burst through the door in a rage. "Sluts!" we hear them shout from our rooms. "What kind of man are you that would allow your daughters to become sluts? Do you even know they bring boys here? Do you know this?"

My sister and I look at each other. Yes, we did have friends, and some were boys. We invited them to the house, even though we knew it was against the rules. But the rules were so backwards. Sometimes, we arranged for friends to come when my aunt was not here. As my father kept long hours at work, we could manage to do things our way. All that was needed was vigilance, a thorough knowledge of his scheduled comings and goings. Baba was clearly outraged that we had taken advantage of the situation; we knew that in his view he had risked his reputation by allowing gaps in his surveillance of us. Thus, the men were loud as they were trying to regain the control that God and the society had given them. Our main concern was that this drama indicated our freedom was at risk. We had not thought past our teenage desire to have fun and hang around with other teenagers. We were so sure that the adults were too busy making each other miserable that they would not notice anything we did.

"You break up your marriage and now your daughters are turning into sluts? You cannot control your women! What kind of man are you?"

Sayeh and I sneak out of our room to get a closer look at what is happening. We crouch on the staircase and can see right into Baba's office. He looks ready to fight them, all of them. The passion of my uncles and their vigorous criticism of my father made this outcome probable. But perhaps because all the men notice us, despite our intention to spy unnoticed, things change. My father and uncles turn on Sayeh and I. We see that one of my uncles is holding a knife and he moves towards us, yelling threats. I race back to our room but Sayeh talks back.

"What are you going to do? Stab me? Go on! You know I am not afraid, and you know you are not going to do it!" She is the rebel like my mom, but she was right. We knew our burly uncles, with their macho moustaches would not hurt us. All they wanted to do was to protect their nieces from boys. They were doing what society said they should do, trying to scare us into behaving properly, concerned that as kids we were not as aware of how a damaged reputation could ruin our futures. It was always the story of shame and *aberoo* (honor). Although we knew we were not in any physical danger and knew that no one would be hurt with the knife our overreacting uncle displays, this was part of the ways women were held back.

In Iran, we say this attitude of men's over-confidence,

dominance, and aggression starts very young and comes from the different way boys and girls are parented. It is rumored that mothers bounce them as infants on their knees, whispering "*doodool tala*" – the literal translation being "golden dick."

With a golden dick, you can do no wrong. Although this is an oversimplification of the narcissism and aggression taught to males, it is a cultural way of describing the communication chasm that starts with raising boys to be gods and raising girls to be beneath them. Yet Sayeh and I were not cowered by their behavior at all. We knew that within a weekend or two, we would manipulate our burly uncles into spoiling us again, lovingly asking us if we needed anything. But how unhealthy is this dance? Men must act macho, and women must react by being silly or childish in order to defuse the situation. After this, Aunt Pari hovers around us to us like we are toddlers and we do not dare to have any male friends over.

Soon my mother cannot handle the badgering and my parents decide to get back together. Maman moves back home, Aunt Pari moves out, and my parents remarry. I am relieved. Some weeks are normal. We host parties, we go up north, Sayeh and I play the piano, Maman and Baba watch and cheer for us. I think everything will be happy and normal, but the peace does not last long. Small things annoy Dad creating rifts between us three females and him. They are replay arguments of the old days—familiar arguments where my mother says she feels constricted, and my father tells her she should be grateful. Except this time, my mom doesn't cry as much. She has worked on herself, but it seems that has made the distance between them greater. It is clearer they have grown apart. A lot of the arguments are about us, Seyah and I, their teenage daughters who are growing up to be, in my father's words, "just like their mother: disobedient and stubborn."

This time, when Maman decides that there was no saving the

Chapter Three

relationship, she takes me and my sister with her. My mother has few housing options as she is a single woman, a divorcee, not an honourable widow. Unfortunately for us all, this move means a great reduction in circumstances, status, income, and happiness.

Chapter Four

You may shoot me with your words,

You may cut me with your eyes,

You may kill me with your hatefulness,

But still, like air, I'll rise.

~ Maya Angelou

A bunch of *khaleh zanak* women are sitting on the ground in front of an apartment building. They are circled around three large, flattened baskets made of colorful plastic: two red ones and a yellow one. Each of these baskets is overflowing with healthy, green herbs which I can smell as we pass: parsley, rosemary, coriander, sage. The herbs come from the vegetable truck that passes every week. These vegetable trucks are part of Tehran's history. People have been utilizing them for generations in these traditional areas of the city.

The five women hunched over together, with two young girls aged eight and five, sit on the sidewalk. The women wear floral cloaks, known as chadors, that cover them from head to toe. One of the children is covered in a white one. The youngest child wears a simple pink t-shirt, blue trousers, and flip flops. They clean the herbs, separating weeds and soil from the fragrant, edible parts as they chat and gossip. My mother never did that. She is classy. We clean our vegetables in our kitchen, or we buy them cleaned from the supermarket. These *khaleh zanak* women have nothing better to do than glare at us through narrowed eyes. Their chatter stops as we pass, but we do not have to be close to them to know what they will say as soon as we are beyond earshot. They sit in judgement of us.

My mom, Sayeh, and I carry shopping bags as we walk to our low-rise apartment. We feel them stare: their unfriendliness says what we know is in their hearts, and to be honest, in our own hearts too. I am sure, had I looked back, I would have seen them rolling their eyes at us. I just know they are thinking *what are those bitches doing here?* I am, however, just as sure that they must be pleased to have found a new topic to gossip about: the new neighbor—an affluent-looking woman with two teenage daughters and no husband. How scandalous!

Chapter Four

The men avoid looking at us directly as this is considered improper. After all, they are true Muslims. They consider themselves to have clean eyes, *cheshm pak*, which they would not dirty by looking at women who are not halal. To them our existence is not lawful or permissible. In the eyes of these *chemsh pak* men and gossipy women, nothing could be as pure and perfect in spirit as them. Thus, their acts of snubbing us and letting us know we were not welcome were to them outward signs of their level of devotion to Allah. Being near them makes me feel naked because I know the rules too. We do not belong in this place *at all*.

I am now sixteen and angry. I ask myself why we had to move away from the neighborhood I knew and loved. Why don't my parents just get along and live peacefully like everyone else's parents? I feel out of place. We do not belong here, but it is what we can afford, Maman tells us, at least for now. Plus, I remind myself that it is close to my high school and I will not have to change schools.

At school, everything is pretty much the same. No one knows where we now live. They assume I am coming and going from my old house. I would be ashamed if they knew that I was not. My close friends knew my parents had divorced again. But I did not want other students to know that I was living in an area with the type of people they would look down on, as they might then look down on me, too.

We continue to get checked randomly, every now and then, by the school administrators. What are they looking for? They are not looking for drugs or real signs of moral decrepitude. Living with a single mother would be construed to be one. No, it is our hair—even under hijab—nails, and eyebrows that are routinely examined. We are not allowed to color our hair or pluck our eyebrows. They check because they know that we are teenagers and that, of course, we want to do these things. It is natural to experiment, to try to be prettier. They make sure our nails are short and unpainted. This is not a problem for me. Mine are always short because I play the piano and guitar.

Our bags get checked also. Cassettes and CDs are also banned. Almost everything is banned: alcohol, drugs, parties, movies with kissing scenes, staying at a hotel room with your boyfriend, dancing in public. The list goes on and on. Everything is banned except, it seems, breathing and mourning. Religious holidays and funerals are the best for those who want to show they are the most devout. They wear black and they cry loud. The louder you can cry and the more dramatic, the better.

Although nearly everything is banned, you can go into a simple home and find a secret wall that opens to reveal hidden stuff, like a James Bond 007 movie. Few people might believe this but in Iran you'll find that the loudest parties, the most expensive alcohols, illegal movies, and even drugs are widely available. Women are dressed spectacularly under their hijabs and chadors. Their hair and makeup as if they are to star in an episode of reality TV's *Keeping Up with the Kardashians*. Men and women gather and dance together. You just have to know where to go and how to bribe the police if you get caught. I learned this as I got older.

For example, like many families, we had a "filmy," someone who delivered rental VHS tapes directly to our house. Each week, we checked the list and let our filmy know which ones we were interested in so he could provide them for us the following week. The filmy had a suitcase full of movies and cartoons. We rented four or five each week. He showed up at an agreed time and day of the week. If he did not, we would know there must have been trouble and that he had most likely been caught by the police. We loved watching movies, but it was illegal. We shared a feeling that we were different from the powers that be. We had to hide our real selves from those living outside of our James Bond world. We needed a James Bond world. It seemed life's simple pleasures were not allowed.

***

One day, as I am walking down the street with my cousin who is also sixteen, we are stopped by the Morality Police. They leap out of a white SUV, with that dreaded green stripe, to question us. Usually, they are looking for hijab infractions. But on this day, my hijab was absolutely perfect, not a strand of hair extended from it. Instead, they want to know more about who I am walking with.

"What is your relationship to this man?" the agent demands.

"We're cousins!" I reply. I can hear my voice shaking. My hands are trembling.

And of course, it does not end at that. We have to take the agents to my mother. Otherwise, we would be in trouble.

Here in Canada, people get into trouble for more serious crimes. In the Tehran of my teenage years, we got into trouble for wearing makeup or using hair dye. We got into trouble for not wearing a hijab properly or exposing our hair. We got into trouble for having parties at home. I grew up in a country where I learned not to voice my opinion or laugh too loudly. I knew it was not fair and I felt it deeply. The rules struck me as stupid. I may have felt defiant inside, but as soon as I saw any vehicle or person I would stiffen and try to be as invisible as possible. There was no way I would defy them like my mother did on occasion when I was a child. I would pray that the threat passed quickly and exhale only when I felt safe again.

Walking with my own male cousin is supposed to be fine;

a relative who is male should not cause such trouble. Yet when I got challenged, every single molecule of courage left me, and I felt like I was doing something wrong. In an atmosphere of fear and terror, honesty can still get you jailed or killed. In Iran, everything is banned, and yet we still keep going. We find ways to enjoy ourselves. People learn how to outsmart the government and the police.

That is how it is.

I am from a culture where girls do not misbehave—at least, not publicly. They don't rise above the cultural norms of the society as conformity is the only way to be safe. The consequences of standing out and being different can be dire. If it is risky to walk down the street with a male cousin, how can young people get to know each other through dating? Dating is not allowed. And to try is risky as the chances of individual actions going unnoticed are small. We are constantly watched. In Islamic law, it is illegal to shake hands with someone of the opposite sex, so it is not surprising that women are not supposed to have sex before marriage or to travel alone.

In Iran, there is this also a kind of fake civility called *târof*. It means that if someone offers you anything, it is impolite to accept it right away. It is quite British, as they might, as would an Iranian, say something like "I couldn't possibly take that!" if offered a delicious pastry no matter how much they wanted it. You have to refuse it at least three times before accepting it. Later my mother-in-law would describe me as rude because I had offered her something only twice. Apparently, I had too quickly accepted her refusal and put the platter down, so she had silently fumed, unable to enjoy that particular treat. And, if you are sitting down, even in the front seat of a car, and someone sits behind you, politeness demands that you apologize to the other person for having your back to them. To which, they must say, "that's okay, a flower has no back." Then, you reply, "a nightingale sits behind the flower." Thus, we are kept in check by *târof*, inspected at school by the superintendent, threatened by family members, and judged on the street by women sitting on the sidewalk cleaning vegetables.

Those gossiping women would have reported us if they observed us making the tiniest rule infraction. Having the official and unofficial Morality Police – my neighbors, teachers, and male relatives— watch us so intensely made me feel as though there was something inherently wrong with me: that I was so bad I had to be checked all the time. As Brené Brown, one of my favorite authors, says, "Shame is the intensely painful feeling or experience of believing that we are flawed and therefore unworthy of love and belonging."

My family was loud and intense, but being watched all the time, even in the name of love and care for us, is invasive. All the scrutiny requires that one always mask their true feelings as being honest about them was risky. When I was in that confusing sphere outside of childhood, due to my family's fear that one slipup could ruin me and them forever, I had to hide the real me in front of family too. Why is everyone so afraid of girls and women? It was like they felt without their eyes on us, we would become like that horrible name that old man called me. How ridiculous that men and society trust us so little.

Women's rights have been restricted since the Islamic Revolution. A man can have as many as four wives in Islam and Sharia Law treats women as half a man. It is legal to compensate women fifty percent less than they would a man in situations such as inheritance and *diyeh*. Diyeh is blood money. If a woman is killed or harmed, the courts might compensate the family with only half of the amount they would give to the heirs of a male victim. Also, a woman's testimony in court is worth only half of a man's and a man can prevent a woman from leaving the country. That thinking permeates the whole society, although I never felt that my family valued me less. It was especially important that us girls obeyed the rules because repercussions outside of the family could not be controlled.

***

To paraphrase Brené Brown, I am the product of a shame-prone culture. I was a "prisoner of pleasing, performing, and perfecting." Even today in Toronto, when I see a jeep of a certain type, I find myself reflexively reaching for my hair, as if to check for a hijab that I no longer wear. The feeling of terror is hard to erase.

I joke with my friends that to have some element of freedom, everyone should know how to drive, bike, and swim. You have to be able to run very fast at times, too. These are survival skills in Iran, necessary so you can be one step ahead of the Morality Police. I learned to swim in the pool at our family house with Maman and Baba and in the Caspian Sea near our villa in Daryakenar. The latter was scary. I heard many stories about how people drowned in the sea. But I worried not. My six uncles, my heroes, were always there.

"Jump, Sara, jump," my uncle, Jamshid, encourages me. "Don't worry. I'm here to catch you. Jump!"

I am hesitant, looking at the size of the pool and the orange floating bands on my tiny arms. I am almost three. Meanwhile, my Uncle Shahin, just seven years older than me, runs and jumps in the pool, splashing water everywhere. My mom, Sayeh, and my uncles wait for me to jump. My dad is filming. There is nothing to be afraid of. Everyone is with me. I jump, and I am like a duck in

Chapter Four

water. They all cheer.

I am safe. I grow up knowing that.

Back then, we could all swim together whether in our family pool or at our villa in Daryakenar, on the Caspian Sea. Unfortunately, after the Islamic Revolution, the rules changed. The men and women's swimming beaches were separated and divided by a fence, respectively.

By the time I was a young adult, I had lost some of the fear, in the way older teenagers often do. My friends and I had tried to outsmart the Morality Police by renting two boats and riding them both far enough in order for the boys and girls to jump in and swim together. We would quickly jump back on board.

Being forced apart also enabled us to find roundabout ways to have fun together. However, we were always plagued by the fear of getting caught by the Morality Police. I was not as adventurous as many. Fear of shaming my parents and disgracing my Baba's name kept me on the female-only side of the beach. And it was the fear of punishment that made me wild that day I made my friend, Omid, jump out the window. The fear of punishment made me force him to jump. My goodness, I think now—that poor boy could have broken his neck in that fall.

"You think you can do whatever you want in this apartment? I just called the Morality Police. You will learn a big lesson today!" my neighbor threatened. And I did.

***

The only fond memories I have from that apartment were the early morning ski trips with other teenagers. I dressed in the darkness of 4:00 am and got into the ski shuttle that picked up all the skiers in the surrounding areas. The loud music in the shuttle woke me up.

During this time, my mother was happier. She underwent self-improvement work. She had also started working as a professional voice actress again. My uncles started to accept the reality that my parents were not getting back together, and their separation was permanent. They realized that no amount of badgering would change my mother's mind. This made it easier for us to visit them.

We saw my father once a month, often in our villa up north in Daryakenar. It was getting easier to accept our new arrangement. Living with my mother in that unpleasant area was bearable knowing I would be seeing my father in our beautiful sea-side cottage. He kept himself busy although he continually complained about indigestion. We insisted he see a doctor and we got shocking news. My Baba was seriously ill. Soon, he needed all of us to take care of him and nurse him to health. I was eighteen when we all moved back with my father, and my parents were unofficially married for the third time. Everything happened so fast, it is hard to remember the timeline. But I do know that within five intense years, cancer would claim his life.

Chapter Five

"Like the magnolia tree,

She bends with the wind,

Trials and tribulation may weather her,

Yet, after the storm her beauty blooms..."

~ Nancy B. Brewer

Pure pink. Pure light. The colors of the flowers on the big magnolia tree in our villa of Daryakenar are warm. The magnolia is the ultimate symbol of happiness to me. It reminds me of my childhood and teenage years: the laughter and tears of my past. It is where I first kissed my first love. It's a tree that even strangers stop to enjoy. Entire families come to admire it and take pictures with it as a backdrop. It was impossible to pass by it without noticing it.

The magnolia tree was situated in the middle of our front yard, in front of the dining room of our country villa, a beautiful, gated complex by the Caspian Sea. We went to Daryakenar for the summer and most holidays. Our villa had a big living room and a dining room. The dining room was big enough to fit a big eight-seat table: one that was full each weekend with family and friends. We were always adding chairs in order to squeeze in more guests. The closets were stuffed with mattresses, futons, and blankets to accommodate everyone. Family and friends visited each weekend as it was only a three-hour drive north of Tehran.

"We live in tribes!" my mom declared as she looked around at each of us squeezed around the table. I loved how she looked. She was joyful. As I reflect back on those gloriously full weekends, I recognize the accuracy in my mother's description of the extended family and community of Iranian life as a tribe. Firstly, we all care about similar things.

We are a small group of people who are connected by a love of food and environment. Secondly, we do not leave home until we get married, and we live close to our parents once we do. Thirdly, we visit our parents often. They become lifetime babysitters to our children. Finally, when it comes to other people raising their kids, making decisions, throwing parties, eating, sleeping, and anything else you can think of, we cannot mind our own business.

Chapter Five

I watched family and friends get drunk, get into arguments, then kiss and make up the next day. We laughed, ate, drank, and told stories. During the summer, our tables were covered with food and surrounded by people sitting closely together. The smell of my mother's dishes stands out as strongly as the magnolia tree.

This is my Daryakenar.

The smell of the food also attracted the stray animals, which were well-fed. I am sure they travelled from villa to villa. Tracy was my black and white cat. I fed her from my plate, despite the protests of my mother. In Iran, stray cats were welcomed more than dogs, which we often shooed away.

"Stay away from those dirty dogs," my uncles said. "They bring diseases. Don't feed them or they will keep coming back."

Those poor dogs missed out as I was unable to feed them in the same way that I did my beloved Tracy. Charcoal barbecued lamb, chicken kebab, or white trout fish freshly bought from the market were grilled by my dad or my uncles. The smell was irresistible which is what drew the dogs to our neighborhood. As I grew older, I often refused to go to the market excursions to buy the food that made our feasts so enjoyable, however my uncles and mother often pleaded with me to join them. Sometimes I submitted but I did not understand why the market was considered such a desirable outing.

"I don't know what you guys like about this market." I said to Maman, pinching my nose with my two fingers. "I can hardly breathe. The whole place smells like fish."

"You won't say that when you eat the yummy *sabzi polo ba mahi*," she replied, while haggling for a discount with the fisherman. "You'll soon forget the smell.

Male villagers sold fish that offended my nose, and older hunchbacked women, with faces deeply wrinkled and browned in the sun, sold freshly picked vegetables that smelled great: mint; leek; parsley; basil; spinach; squash; pumpkins; onions; garlic; carrots; green beans; fava beans; cucumbers; scallions; tomatoes; and eggplant. Once purchased, they were washed, cut, and chopped. It was a gruelling job that I was co-opted into at age twelve.

The reward of playing by the Caspian Sea was worth every minute I spent in vegetable drudgery. Every day was beach day in the summer. The women-only beaches were surrounded by an ugly plastic barricade, which was intended to divide and separate our swimming area from the men. It seemed rather silly to me, especially since men on the boats cruised around and were able watch us from afar. We made sandcastles when we were kids and worked on our tans when we got older. Risking a sunburn was the price of beauty and we happily paid it. We interrupted our tanning for meals of rice and fish or chicken BBQ, then finished off the day playing cards or charades.

My mother never had many rules for us. As teenagers, we did not update her on our every move, unlike most other girls our age who fielded questions from their moms every ten to twenty minutes. They were constantly required to check-in with their parents. "Why don't you call us when we go up north?" I once asked my mother. I wondered if her relaxed attitude meant that she did not care as much.

"I know you are safe. I trust it. If something happens, I figure someone will call and tell me. If I get no call, that means I have nothing to worry about!"

Unlike many traditional Persian mothers, mine trusted me. She did not need constant reassurance and she didn't keep me so close that I had no room to grow. Consider her advice about men,

Chapter Five

"A woman should date at least three different guys at the same time. One to go and watch a movie with, one to sleep with, and one to have deep conversations with."

My eyes grew as big as a tarsier. I could not believe my ears. I laughed in shock when she said this. Afterall, we lived in a country where you were not even allowed to go on dates with someone of the opposite sex. I would risk being caught by the Morality Police for daring to go out with a male, yet my mother was suggesting that I date not one but three.

Having such a bold and brave free thinker for a mother set a foundation that would eventually help me break free of shame for being a sexual woman. Still, the ever-present feeling that countered the spirited confidence I received from my mother was fear. I was afraid of disgracing my dad's name. "Don't let the guys chase you like stray dogs! Value yourself! What would people think?" my dad would say. He was always on alert for signs of behavior that could ruin his reputation.

Daryakenar was where all the cool teenagers hung out each summer. It was the only place to run around with boys. We sailed to deeper water, away from the eyes of the Morality Police, in order to swim, boys and girls together. We sat on stone walls sipping milkshakes in the evenings. Chasing boys becomes our favourite thing. Our second favourite was playing hard-to-get and hoping they would chase us. Isn't that what all teenagers do?

We were no different than Canadian teenagers. But unlike Canadian teens, we were under threat at all times. We had to be aware of every vehicle that passed through our gated community, of every person who came and went. We took some comfort in the fact that non-residents were not able to enter the area. But of course, the Morality Police knew how to bypass this supposed security and ruin the fun for us.

One evening, we sat on the stone wall, chatting as we sipped our milkshakes and looking at boys who checked us out. All of a sudden, I heard screaming. I then saw people running in different directions. The Morality Police were chasing people for no discernable reason and beating them with sticks. I threw down my milkshake and ran towards my villa. As the Persian expression goes, I ran so fast that it was as if I borrowed another pair of legs. I ran without looking back. I was covered in sweat and propelled by my terror of getting caught and beaten. I grew tired, but I knew I was getting close to the villa and mustered up the strength to continue, I concentrated on the sound of my feet hitting the ground. I could not bring in enough air to fill my lungs, but I could not slow down, and although I was aware that the screams sounded distant, I could not be sure that no one was chasing me. I kept running despite the pain in my lungs as I gasped for air.

It was then that I saw my neighbor's dog, a Doberman, that had always made me nervous. It started towards me. The Doberman was free from his usual chain tying him to his owner's property. It came after me, chasing, barking, and growling, I ran even faster. I had no choice. I had an additional reason to be terrified. A blessing that made it possible for me to run harder.

When I got to our villa, I burst through the door and swung it closed behind me. I was safe. As I leaned against the closed door, trying to catch my breath, a wave of nausea made me retch. I threw up the milk shake. I was in such fear that I cried for an hour. My father never knew, or he would have prevented me from ever sitting on that stone wall with friends again.

Unlike the freedom and trust offered by my mother, my father made black and white rules for me. Despite how strict he was, his redeeming quality was his great sense of humor. He loved to tell jokes and mimic actors. At the same time, he expected straight

Chapter Five

A's on our school report cards. He insisted that we did not wear short skirts or make-up, go to parties, and have boyfriends. We did our best to comply, but we were adventurous and had a cheeky rebellious streak. We kept a whole lot of secrets from him with Maman's help.

Obviously, he wanted the best for us. He invested in our education and hired tutors to help us with our lessons. It was hard to get him to invest in the other things that our friends had, things that we considered necessities. It took us years to convince him to buy a new car, a TV set, or furniture. He was strategic with money, like so many other Persian men. He bought properties out in what I considered the boonies. He would say, "You don't get it now. You will thank me in the future." And he was right. The remote areas where he purchased investment properties are now developed and over-priced. We eventually benefitted from the investments we doubted, including our lovely villa in Daryakenar.

This place in northern Iran was our safe getaway place. We have entire photo albums full of pictures from our time in the north. My father loved it so much that he built his movie theatre there. But movie theatres were doomed to die after the Revolution. The content of the films were considered not Islamic and were a common target of rioters. They tried to scare people away from anything considered too Western.

One of the bigger secrets I kept from my father was my friendship with Leila. She was one of the coolest girls in the neighbourhood. Guys liked her, and I watched as they did anything to impress her. She was beautiful, confident, and smart. In fact, girls also tried to impress her, hoping to get close to her and to be invited into her inner circle. I usually went to her to ask questions about dating. Eventually she and I became quite close. "You can't let guys have you easy! Make them work hard to have you," Leila advised.

I wondered how she could date several guys and party hard yet get good grades at the same time. But eventually, even Leila settled down. The coolest girl on the block fell for the coolest guy in the neighborhood. They dated for over a year. She called him "the one."

One day, Leila called me. Her voice was shaking.

"Is something up? I can hardly hear you."

She started sobbing. "Sara, please come. I can...cannot talk...on the phone. Please can you come now?" She hung up.

What's going on? I wondered as I rushed over. Did they get caught by the police? Has someone died? Did they break up?

She opened the door as soon as she saw me arrive. She looked pale. Her eyes had already puffed up from crying.

"You…you can't tell…tell anybody. Promise?" she stuttered.

She was terrified. My heart started beating fast. Suddenly, I knew what the problem was. I looked at her and my mouth opened in shock.

"Are you pregnant?" I blurted out.

"Yes," she said.

The next few weeks were a nightmare. Nobody could know. Nobody. Not my father. Not even my mother. The coolest girl on the block was in trouble and she had no one but me to help her get out of it. Because the repercussions are so dire, there are no teen pregnancies in Iran. Abortion is against the law throughout Iran and a pregnancy before marriage is a huge, huge shame. Finding a gynaecologist willing to break the law and provide Leila with an abortion would be difficult, expensive, and incredibly risky. I did not know what the punishment of such a crime for Leila and for the doctor could be, but I was certainly afraid for them and for myself.

Leila broke up with her boyfriend and managed to find someone to perform the abortion. It cost her a huge amount of money. She borrowed it in secret, from a guy we trusted who was just a bit older than us. This solution was not available to most women, but Leila, through this guy, found a private clinic that performed the abortion after their working hours. I went with her and it was one of the scariest things I have ever done. We were both terrified, but this was the only option there was to save Leila's reputation, and, we thought, maybe even her life.

She was traumatized and became a different person afterward. She was no longer the vibrant party-girl. She also wanted nothing more to do with me. After her abortion, she had only one goal: to get out of Iran as soon as she could. I shared that goal. Everything seemed much more complicated than it needed to be. We lived in a haze of secrets and lies. Although losing your virginity meant you could be impregnated like Leila, and that you would supposedly have difficulty finding a husband, most teenagers were having sex.

If a relationship ended and women needed to cover up their loss of virginity, they had to find a gynecologist to stitch their vagina tighter, so as to seem like they had never had sex. This was done in an effort to fool a future husband, particularly a traditional one. This is another one of our secrets. Non-virgins get stitched back regularly in Iran, as if they are a hole in a sock.

I did not like the idea of stitching or marrying a narrow-minded guy. Although I fooled around, I did not have sex until I was in my twenties. Every time I came close to losing my virginity, I thought of Leila and I made some excuse to get out of the situation.

***

Shomal means north. This describes the area my father loved, an area which encompasses Daryakenar. It is green and beautiful. In Daryakenar, another well-known and loved feature is the pink and purple papery flowers—bougainvilleas—that hang from the walls of villas and other buildings. Here, it rains a lot, similar to the west coast of Canada. It gets pretty hot and humid in the summer and cool and romantic in fall. When it's windy, and it pours, it is nasty and spooky, a true contrast to its usual beauty. Our villa in Daryakenar was far-enough away from Tehran to become a haven to us when the chaos and violence of the Iran-Iraq War ensued. The war –that was originally fought at the Iran-Iraq border – managed to reach our relative safe city of Tehran.

The war lasted eight years, starting in 1980, only a year after the end of the Islamic Revolution of 1979. A treaty for peace was signed in 1988. For two months in 1985, we were in serious danger although throughout it we faced shortages in medicine, toothpaste, and car parts. Food was rationed. The news outlets reported that our soldiers were fighting valiantly to keep Iraq from seizing territory that had been in dispute for generations. It was a complete surprise to us all when the Iraq air force dared to move inland and fire on Tehran.

I will never forget the day we heard the air sirens over our radios followed by the announcers barking: *"Tavajoh! Tavajoh!* The siren you are hearing indicates that an air strike will take place immediately. Please take shelter."

I was only ten. I completely panicked, but my parents knew what to do. "To the basement!" My father called to us. "Run!" We rushed, bumping into each other as we descended down our narrow stairs, enveloped by the sound of sirens and the screams of other families who had fled from their homes and into the street.

Chapter Five

In their panic, they were trying to outrun the bombs, but the explosions were so loud that they could not tell which direction they came from.

If sirens woke us at night, we had no time to make it to the basement. We stood in the door frames, away from the windows, praying as bombs dropped around us. The piercing of the sirens stopped only when it was certain that the danger had subsided. The danger only subsided when the Iraqi jets were either shot down by our soldiers or retreated back the way they came.

Living through the threat of raids meant that we needed to keep all of our lights off at night. The blackouts were almost as scary as the air raids themselves. We laid in darkness, anticipating the sound of air raids. I still do not know how anyone could sleep in such an intense state of anticipation. We laid down together in one room, our muscles tense, and waited for an instruction to run to the basement.

When the air raids first began in Tehran, there were nights when we drove an hour away and waited in our car. We returned home when it was safe. However, it was soon clear that the wisest option was to head north and stay at our villa. When we left for Daryakenar, we had no idea how long we would have to be away. We wondered if our house in Tehran was blasted into rubble, like many of the homes around us.

Only one of my uncles was called up as soldiers, as were most men of fighting age. Children became soldiers too. While we hid in Daryakenar, one of our uncles called to say that a missile had just missed our home. When it exploded, its force shattered most of our windows. Baba rushed back to Tehran the following day to make repairs to the house.

Uncle Hamid, served on the front line, near the border and

remains haunted by the amount of death he witnessed. "I once jumped into a grave, lying down on dead bodies during an attack." He is unable to talk about his experiences during that time.

We were lucky that our uncle survived. There are still many missing soldiers and civilians. The war is fresh in the minds of people living in Iran. Whole towns were obliterated. One town, called Dezful, had the record of having been bombed the most during the early part of the war. On a particularly hot day, Iraqi missiles hit when most people were in their cooler basements. There are so many stories of the carnage. Only body parts were found afterwards. Too many. There are too many still-missing people wiped out like this.

***

Five years after the end of the war, when I was eighteen and just when we learned that my father was ill, I started a two-year course at a university in Babol. My grades were not good enough for me to gain entrance to programs in universities in Tehran. In order to study computer science at university, my uncles had decided it was best for me to study math in high school. To them, it did not matter that I hated math. They were the leaders of our tribe and they decided how I had to lead my life. The days of straight A's ended when my parents first separated. I received my first failing grade in algebra just before we moved into the apartment without my father. I was never able to maintain straight A's after that.

In Iran, prospective university students take a competitive entrance exam. A high score gives the student more choice in terms of both university and course selection. My score was not high enough to grant me entrance into the best university in Tehran. When it came to program selection, I hid my choices from my family to ensure they had no power to force a change. I did not want to study computer science, so it did not matter that I was not

Chapter Five

eligible to study it. Instead, I studied medical laboratory science.

My dad was excited when he found out that I was accepted to a university close to both our villa and his cinema. He even admired my chosen field of study. He said, "Continue your education and get your PhD in that field. You'll be a doctor."

I took taxi cabs back and forth from Daryakenar to my university while others took buses. I hated buses. They were packed and stinky and extremely slow, stopping every five minutes to drop off or pick up slow moving, unperfumed country folk. Not for me. I didn't have time for these people who were, to me, living in a different world. They were too chilled and laid-back. I was in a hurry as I was doing important stuff.

I was my daddy's little princess. And I chose to pay the extra to get into those cabs. We only had to wait for an additional three passengers to show up and squeeze in the cab rather than squeeze into a bus of fifty. If I was lucky, I would get the front seat all to myself while the other three were squashed in the back. Thinking back, I understood that meant the smallest one was sitting in the large passenger front seat!

I felt independent by making choices for myself. However, I was only as autonomous as the times would permit. My father visited often and although I knew he was sick, his illness did not seem serious to us. Aunt Pari needed a new place to live so it was decided she would move to ensure I behaved myself. When she moved in to take care of me, she made sure I knew that she was doing me a tremendous favor. She cooked and managed the villa. It felt like déjà vu from my parents' first separation. I made sure to avoid Aunt Pari as much as I could. When she would ask me what I would like to eat, I told her that I had already eaten at the university. I resisted her hovering shadow. It sought to suck up my independence.

Aunt Pari was not the only one who helped my father make sure I remained a good girl. My neighbors spied on me and reported to my father. One day, a neighbor saw me arrive home from my boyfriend's villa. "I'm watching you!" he said. "I don't think you want me to tell your father what I think you are doing here!"

Even though I was now a young adult, I had to be very careful. I realized just how watched I was. People knew who my father was because he had owned the villa for a long time. He was also the owner of the cinema. Plus, if they did business with my father, or if they served us in their restaurants, he would tip them generously. They respected him. I had to be careful as I too was well known. I did not want to shame my dad.

I met my first serious boyfriend, Iman, in university. Iman was tall and handsome, with big dark eyes. He was charming and open-minded. At least, at first, he appeared to be. He seemed different from other guys. He made my life interesting while I was living up north, as he was staying at his parents' villa in Daryakenar, too.

We did not have the wild college experience depicted in the North American and European media. Whenever I watched movies about American students having fun in college, I envied them. For us, university life was about studying. The most I did, other than studying, was have dinner with my boyfriend. Well, it was a bit more than that, I admit. But everything was done in secret. I could not be open about our relationship and how beautiful I felt when I was with him. This was as risqué as university life got for us. There was no dancing in bikinis or spring break getaways. That's for sure.

Iman and I kissed for the first time under the magnolia tree. I was nineteen and in love; I thought he would be the love of my life. Two years later, I cried my eyes out as I sat alone in my bedroom. That I discovered he was not as supportive of women as I initially thought should have been a clue that the relationship would fail.

Chapter Five

A bigger clue, one that I chose to ignore, was that my mother told me to dump him as soon she met him. She just knew, she said. She just knew.

My mother and I were invited to meet his parents in Tehran. After spending less than an hour with them, she whispered that the relationship would never work. I tried to hush her, concerned they would hear her. "Sara, look! They are too traditional for you. You will not fit in with this family." At first, I chose to ignore her. He was my first serious boyfriend and I wanted it to turn out right. When it became more and more obvious that his family did not like me, we broke up.

"How did this happen? Two years of my life wasted," I told myself. I had been so sure he was the one. I wailed even though, in my heart, I knew our decision to part was the right one.

Iman was not my first boyfriend, however. That honour went to Ali, a boy I met at a party when I was seventeen. This was during the time when my parents were separated. My sister and I lived with my mother. In the middle of the night, while Maman was sleeping, I snuck Ali into my bedroom. Ali and I fooled around, but it was Iman who I decided to lose my virginity to.

Deciding to have sex before marriage was a big deal. I used protection, but instead of focusing on pleasure, I was worried about the what ifs. What if we get caught? What if the condom breaks? What if I get pregnant? What if I have to seek an abortion? What if my father finds out? What if it ruins my life? My future? My marriage?

But Iman! Iman! I wailed in those days after we broke up. In my time of grief, it brought no relief that the decision was mutual. After all, he was with me as I recovered from my nose job. Like many Persian women, I was convinced that all I needed to look beautiful was to have one of those straight, sloped, European noses. We are not socialized to appreciate the big, humped noses that come with our Middle Eastern blood. Many girls are casually asked "when do you want to get your nose done?" because in Iran, it is a rite of passage, like getting your period or your first bra. Iman was there for me. He drove me home after my surgery, careful to avoid any potholes. Sudden bumps could cause excessive bleeding. He even fed me pineapples to help reduce puffiness and bruising around my eyes.

Now Iman was gone, although he remained part of my warm memories of Daryakenar, an inseparable part of my life. Thinking of Daryakenar fills me with memories of family bonds, love, friendships, and innocence. It conjures up the smell of lime trees, jasmine, daffodils, pine trees, burned wood, and barbecue. The power of waves splashing against rocks, the bike paths, ghost stories, and secrets: these remind me of the magic of my younger years. The beauty of magnolias is forever my favourite with their deep colors and delicate flowers. Many significant events took place with the magnolia tree as a backdrop. It was not long after my breakup with Imam when I kissed another man under it. This time, the man and I would marry.

Chapter Six

"I wish I could show you when you are lonely

or in darkness the astonishing light of your own being."

~ Hafez

Little Sara of Tehran

I am driving my big SUV. It is not really mine, but I drive it so frequently that it feels like mine. It belongs to my parents. It's half purple, half silver, and eye-catching. I see a similarly cool car. It's a black Opel, a German luxury car. Through the mirrors, I see that its good-looking driver is staring at me. Our eyes meet in the mirrors and I know he is following me. This is how we flirt in Tehran, although in Canada, someone following you is reason to call the police! We were close enough that I could use car mirrors to give him the "look." It's the look to show an interest in a guy, so he can see that this game of him following me is worth his time.

I see, in the rear-view mirror, that he follows as I pull over and park my car in a small strip mall. I head to the pharmacy without looking back. We meet inside. He's short, but I do not care as I am Little Sara, one of the smallest people in the world, and I am looking good. I never leave the house without some make-up. My hair is shoulder length, covered by a mandatory hijab. I choose the most beautiful fabrics I can find. It has a chiffon-like fabric in shades of blue and green draped in a way that would look fashionable in London or Paris. The way I've arranged my hijab over my head and shoulders is casually chic; it resembles something Audrey Hepburn would wear, as I've arranged it to look almost like a shawl and it is so suitable to this cool, cloudy day. My hijab covers my throat and shoulders, and I am dressed in a dark, navy blue manto.

He introduces himself. His name is Bahador, and he is on his way to meet friends at a cafe. He mentions its name and I recognize it as a modern lively, popular place that everyone frequents. He casually drops that he is studying law at Azad University, an expensive private school. It's well-known as many of the rich families send their kids there. It does not impress me much. It's easier to get into Azad University than most public universities; all it takes is money. Bahador is cocky. He's studying law and is close to graduation. Soon he will be a lawyer.

Chapter Six

"I had better get on my way. My parents will be concerned," I say when my flirting senses tell me that leaving at this point will have the greatest impact on him. My instincts are right. He genuinely does not want me to go. I feel something. I like him. He is the first man I've felt anything for since Iman. He scribbles his name and phone number on a piece of paper and hands it to me slowly, forcing me to almost tug it from his hand. I smile and shake my head. I glance up at him through my thick lashes. I know that my eyes are one of my best features.

I look away, carefully putting the important slip of paper into my handbag. I feel chills and it is as though there is a bubble around us. The sounds of parents with kids and other shoppers blur as if they are under water. The extended leg of the toddler hits my arm. The mother looks back at me, as if she has done something wrong. I take a deep breath and move a step away from Bahador. "Manzoori nadaashtam," she says. *Sorry!* She smiles and I smile back. I am grateful to be brought back into the real world, released from the magnetism of this man.

"Will you call me?" he asks. I can hear the confidence in his voice. He assumes any woman, given the chance, would die to be on his arms. *Doodool tala*? Maybe. But he is going places and has much to offer so in many ways, I figure, his arrogance is earned.

"Sorry," I say, "but I don't normally call random people I meet on the street."

I want to call Bahador, but I know I cannot. To call him seems desperate. But I figure I can arrange an accidental meet-up. We both live in the same neighborhood. I leave and I know that his eyes are watching me. I turn back and give him that look one more time. I know what I am doing.

Two weeks later, I am heading up north to Daryakenar in

my purple-silver SUV. I am driving and chatting with my friend, Hamideh, who sits in the back seat. My mom is seated next to me in the passenger seat. She laughs so hard and makes fun of us while we discuss all the things of interest to young women in Iran: men, life's restrictions, the trendiest fashions, the coolest places to meet, plus, of course, the latest gossip about childhood friends.

It is summertime and the roads leading up to Daryakenar are busy. The drive takes much longer than usual, so as soon as we get to Daryakenar, we drive to a café to grab a bite to eat. Hamideh and I sit at a table, enjoying our iced coffee at a seaside table. My mother wanders off to buy something for tonight's meal. We survey the people walking by. We wear dark sunglasses to disguise our stares.

A tall guy approaches our table and my friend leans forward. I look up and recognize his shorter friend, a few steps behind him. It is Bahador. He brightens as he has just spotted me. "What a coincidence! You have a villa here?" he asks, without trying to hide his excitement.

"Yes, we do." My dark sunglasses help me keep the façade of being unfazed.

"We do, too! We're neighbors here and in Tehran! How come we had never seen each other here before?" Because we're both small people getting lost in the crowd, I think in my head. I smile and before I can even think of anything witty in reply, he continues: "You never called."

"I told you I wouldn't."

He smiles, shakes his head, and gives a little snort. He gets it. I introduce him and his friend to Hamideh just as my mother returns. Hamideh is elbowing me, trying to hint at me to not to let this go. I guess she likes his tall, skinny friend with his northern

Chapter Six

accent.

Bahador gives me his phone number again and says, "I'd like to see you." This time he is not asking a question.

I tip my head to one side, as if saying "we'll see." They leave and we watch them disappear. I notice that my mother has returned and is watching us as we watch them. We all dissolve into giggles. Maman takes her seat and wags her fingers at us, as if to say, "be good." She smiles. Hamideh and I talk over each other, trying to convince her that these boys are interested in us and that we have them under our control.

"Girls," Maman says in mock-exasperation, "remember my advice: three boys! Date three," she counts on her fingers for emphasis. "One to go to the movies with, one to sleep with, one to have deep conversations with. Those *doodool tala*? I am not sure those boys are worth any of these."

***

The next morning, my friend and I get into the car to go for a spin. The car does not start. My mom comes out to give us a hand. She gets in the driver's seat, but she does not know any more about cars than I do. Maman rummages in her purse. She wants to call the local mechanic: "What is the name of the guy? Remember him? He owns the shop we went to last year when we had to get a new tire. That guy was shorter than you, Sara!" I know she is looking for her leather-bound blue address book. She has had it for as long as I can remember.

"Hold on," I say. A big naughty smile spreads on my face. "I know who we can call." Here's the time to call Bahador and see how much he can help. "Let's see if he's a man," I say. Hamideh and my mother know exactly what I am up to.

Bahador shows up within ten minutes. He wears jeans and a crisply ironed light blue shirt, open at the throat. It's hot and humid but he looks cool and unbothered by the weather. He lifts up the hood and looks at the engine, rolling up his sleeves. He fumbles around and I see that he gets his hands dirty. He says with that confidence again: "The battery is calcified. It will need to be replaced. For today, let's jump start the battery."

I just about died, right there on the spot. He's the guy, I decide. He is confident. He's handy. He's not afraid to do just a little bit of work, to get his hands dirty. He's intelligent, educated, and charming. I agree to go out on a date with him.

After a couple of weeks, we start to see each other every day. He has just finished law school and he is studying to get into the master program. He has the time to treat me like the princess I am, and he does. He drives me to Iran University each day and he takes me out to cafes and restaurants. After I finish my two-year associate degree, I pass another entrance exam and work towards my Bachelor of Science degree. This is not a short drive, but he is willing to do this for me. When he cannot drive me, he lets me drive his beloved Opel. I am falling for him and he has already told me he loves me. He is a real man, I tell myself. I am his helpless angel. That's how we date in Iran. These are the roles we fulfill: A real man and a helpless angel.

I feel that we are perfect together.

One day, I am driving Bahador's Opel with a friend and someone hits us from the side. My heart starts pounding. We are lucky to be uninjured. I am unsure of how to call Bahador to break the news that his beloved brand-new, meticulously clean vehicle is damaged.

What if he gets angry? I ask myself. I am reminded of the fury

Chapter Six

I am used to witnessing from my father and my uncles. What will he say to me? What will he tell his parents?

He is quiet during the call and tells me he will come to collect me shortly. When he picks me up in a different beautiful car, he does not say much. He drives me to my house, and hardly responds as I continuously apologize. When I shut the car door carefully, I lean in through the open window, weeping. "Please forgive me!" I beg. I wonder if I will lose him. I watch him drive away.

Within a few hours he calls to tell me he told his parents it was him who got into the accident. He forgives me without a show of anger. I love him even more.

When we can, we sneak out to the little room on the rooftop of the apartment where he lives with his parents to make out. We are careful. We do not want his parents to find out that we are seeing each other all the time. They are a typical traditional family that expects their eldest and most responsible son to marry a virgin or, as we say in Iran, *aftab-mahtab nadideh* meaning "one who has not been glimpsed by the sun or moon." If we are to be married, they must never know that we have been spending this much unsupervised time together.

Bahador and I date for three years, trying to make it seem as though we are just casual friends in an effort to hide our relationship from our parents. He says we should marry once he finishes his master's degree in law. I am working on being a supportive girlfriend. I am always available when he calls, and I listen intently as he describes his life as a student and his dreams for our future.

After getting my degree, I land a position in a hospital as an intern working in a medical lab. I am good at what I do. Most of my work is in the hematology department where I diagnose cancerous cells. My heart breaks whenever I think of what the families go through after receiving the results of the tests that I run. I cannot truly feel the depth of sadness that they must feel until my own family goes through this same experience.

"Adenocarcinoma colon cancer," I read on Baba's pathology report. How could I, daddy's little princess, find the courage to deliver this bad news to my father and my family? My father was more ill than I thought. I could no longer pretend that he would get better. When I saw his report, prepared by a colleague, I gulped hard, holding back tears. With my years of schooling and experience, I knew the outcome, but I was not going to let mere statistics and probabilities remove my hope. I consulted with doctors at the hospital. Then, I sought the top doctors in Iran and asked about experimental trials.

We managed to get my father preferential treatment. He did not wait as long for medical attention as other patients. He got the best room when he was admitted. He received the best nursing care at home because now he was always sick and went to the hospital only on the advice of the nurse, or when we felt we could not handle things at home. The nurses, however, were rarely needed because of my uncles.

At home, my uncles nursed him, and bathed him as his health got worse, allowing my mother and I to just love him while they did most of the hard work. This was one of the greatest gifts anyone could give another person. It allowed my mother and I to come to terms with the end of his life. We had a whole support team and he lacked for nothing. My sister had moved to Canada and we stayed connected by telephone and email.

My beautiful Baba fought his cancer for five years, and all the while, he did not lose his sense of humor. He started balding at a young age and had lost most of his hair even before he got married,

Chapter Six

"See! I lost all of my hair because of the chemo," he joked.

A few months before his death, I sat beside him as he lay in bed. He was getting weaker and weaker. "Are you guys going to marry or what?" I was struck silent. How did he know? "You can't just keep seeing each other like this forever," he continued. "Break up or get married. It is time to make things official and right."

Maman shrugged and hardly looked up from the book she was reading. "Really, I see no reason to rush," she said. Later, when it is just the two of us, she warns me against marriage to Bahador, just as she warned me against marrying Iman. "Sara, I don't think he is the man for you. That family will not want you for their son. And you know, just like your father, that family will make sure you are not able to work as soon as you are married. You are not meant for that life, Little Sara."

I insist that just because they are traditional and a bit too religious that this does not mean Bahador's a bad guy. We can all get along, I've decided. I was in love and my mother's words could not dim my desire for a future with Bahador. My father was ill and wanted to make sure that I would be a respected woman in the community rather than hang on as an illicit girlfriend. I watched my father go from being a strict, strong man, to a weak, vulnerable one who I loved but did not know. His demanding that I get married was a good sign as it showed he was not consumed by his illness; he was still watching out for me. Baba could not be ignored. We needed to start making plans.

***

My mom and I took Baba for his chemo and stayed at the hospital for his surgeries. I witnessed just how physically devastating cancer and its treatment can be. After one particular surgery, where they removed the lower part of my dear Baba's intestines, they removed the full rectum and created an alternate opening for waste on his stomach. I had to clean my father's wounds. Despite our care, it became infected. Every single time that I cleaned it, I teared up, but never let him see my distress.

"It is getting better, yes Sara?" he asked.

"Yes, much better, dad," I'd lie. "You'll soon be able to get rid of the colostomy bag."

He cried as I helped him change his colostomy bag, attaching it to this new opening on his belly. "I never thought I would be so helpless and weak. Now my daughter sees my poop in a bag."

I still cry thinking about that.

I prayed for a miracle. "God, heal him or take him," was my prayer. He was suffering too much. Even morphine did little to numb his pain. We went to the hospital and they ran more tests as he was not improving. I remember seeing black dots all over his lung x-rays.

"Just take him home, we can't do much for him," his doctor said as if he were talking about a shoe, rather than my father.

We did. My mom, sister, uncles, Aunt Pari, and I took my beloved father home and watched him die, the life draining out of him little by little yet still this was faster than I thought I could bear. In his last days, he was skeletal. His facial bones stuck out from his fleshless, thin skin. He would stare with sunken eyes at the ceiling, as if he was talking to someone up there. Angels, maybe. Perhaps his father or mother. It was difficult to witness this change in him. He had always been powerful, confident, strong, and authoritative throughout this life.

"I love you," he said to my mother while he was holding her hand a few days before he died. Despite the fights and the divorces,

Chapter Six

those were some of his last words.

"Look after Sara and watch Bahador when I'm gone. I don't want her to get hurt," my dad requested of Uncle Shahin. I was his little girl even when he was suffering.

"His lungs are full of water. You need to prepare yourselves the worst," the nurse said only a week after our last visit to the hospital. She paused, her eyes full of sympathy. "He might not make it through the night."

We all sat with him and by 3:00am, he was gone. I heard sobbing and screaming swell throughout the house. I called Bahador and he came over immediately. Shahin gave him a cold look for this intrusion, but he looked at me and then realized I needed him.

It did not take long for the ambulance to arrive. In a short time, my dad's body was wrapped in a white cloth, placed on a stretcher. All I could hear was my uncles and our neighbor's chants of "Allah o akbar. Allah o akbar" as they carefully maneuvered the stretcher with my father's body on it out of the house and into the waiting ambulance.

My father lost his life to cancer when I was twenty-four, a few months before I was to get married. My engagement was a sad time. It was also a great distraction from the Baba-sized hole in my heart. I planned for my future, but the deep grief of losing my father kept me in my past. Some days, I could not get out of bed and I would stay under the covers and cry all day. The only time I felt normal was when I was asleep. Sometimes, I took medication to help me stay asleep. Sleep was my great escape.

I learned that Bahador had come and asked to speak to my dad before he died. He assured my barely conscious father that I would be taken care of, telling him, "I am going to marry your daughter." I was happy to hear this. It showed his respect and love for me.

After my father died, Bahador's family visited mine to formally ask for my hand in marriage. My grandfather was there to act on behalf of my father. The engagement tradition is for the groom's family to visit the bride-to-be's family. Most of the family is at this gathering. We had my mother and grandfather, plus older relatives, including my two uncles. As expected, Bahador visited with his parents and his sister. His sister wore a full-black chador. The only things visible were her hands and face. My sister, my mother, and I never dressed like that and were taken aback by this formal display of devoutness in a rather casual family setting. His mom wore a casual scarf.

In order to protect me, my uncles had been asked around, investigating Bahador's family. My uncle, Mehrad, came to me. "Did you know that Bahador has five other brothers and sisters besides those here?" he asked.

It was a total shock to me. I did not know what to say and for a moment, my breath stopped. I finally inhaled deeply, I hoped imperceptibly. I tried to calm my pacing heart.

"Yes. Of course, I know that." I replied.

It turned out that Bahador's father had been married before. The five other siblings were from his first marriage. I knew of these people, but I had no idea they were Bahador's stepsiblings. In fact, I remembered that together, Bahador and I had visited one of the sisters in hospital when she was gravely ill. He had told me she was his cousin.

"Why would you lie to me?" I later asked Bahador. "Do you know how it felt that my own uncle was the one to tell me? And that I had to pretend to know? We were in the hospital with her, and you couldn't even tell me then? You told me your sister was your cousin! Why and how could you deny her?"

"I didn't want to lose you!" Bahador cried.

To him, it made complete sense to try to keep his father's other family secret. He was ashamed that he was a part of his father's second family, rather than the first. He was also ashamed of what had happened between his parents. When his parents first started to live together, his father was still married to his first wife, which is perfectly legal in Iran as a man can have up to four wives. I learned that the reason Bahador's mother had so many children, so close in age, was because since the first wife had five children, she wanted to have as many. His mother wanted to be sure that when his father died, she would get half of his money, just like the first wife.

This worried me.

But I was engaged already.

Not long after my father's funeral, Bahador's mother asked if my father had left the Daryakenar villa to me although she already knew that to be true.

"My dear, Sara," she said, "you won't need two cottages in that area. We have one, too. Why don't you sell that cottage and buy my son a Mercedes? His other one is getting old. You love him so much. Don't you think you should do that?"

My father had just died, and she was already asking me to give them his money? My grief was still fresh, yet she suggested I sell a place so dear to my family in order to give her son another car. "We aren't married yet," is all I could bring myself to say.

My mother was not happy about the engagement. She felt I

was making a mistake. She was in no hurry to take any steps to make this mistake a more permanent one. However, it was not in her nature to badger me about it. She made it clear that she was there for me no matter what. But as she could not be a hypocrite, she did not offer to be part of some of the traditional preparations for a ceremony.

It is traditional for Iranian mothers to help choose their daughters' engagement rings and shop for a new home. My mother was not interested in what I put on my finger or how I furnished our home. Most importantly, she wanted to make sure I was not getting married to cover up my grief. Instead of shopping, she stayed with me 24/7.

My uncles felt my mother should have put her feelings aside to prepare for my impending marriage. I was in no condition to be critical of my mother, especially after losing my father. She had lost her husband too. Despite their two divorces, they had been in each other's lives for twenty-eight years. When I pointed this out, my uncles understood and did not grumble with as much intensity as they usually would. Instead, they went shopping with me. Although Bahador's family had plenty of money and bragged about it constantly, I knew they were close-fisted and cheap. I wanted them to see that I fit in with the family, therefore whatever I chose was not expensive.

When my mother saw the simple fabrics selected for my wedding gown, she said, "Seriously, Sara? With all the money they are so proud to tell everyone that they have, you are choosing this?"

I said nothing. It was obvious that she did not understand. Instead, I told her how happy I was that I found a tailor who did not charge much to make my wedding dress. To me, it was important that Bahador and his family knew that I was not interested in money and I could demonstrate this by refusing the *mehrieh*.

Chapter Six

The *mehrieh* is a payment, often in gold coins, that is given by the groom's family to the bride. I made it clear, I wanted no part of such a patriarchal practice.

"Imagine! It is like you would be buying me!" I said to Bahador as we lay in bed together. "There is no way I would do that. It is so old-fashioned."

Bahador told this to his family and during the pre-engagement family meeting, they suggested there be no gold coins. When they saw the shock on my family's faces, they realized the huge mistake they had made, and immediately accepted a *merieh* of six hundred gold coins proposed by my grandfather. The normal agreement for gold coins is equal to the Persian year of the bride's birth. My Persian birth year is 1354 meaning they should have offered that many gold coins. Six hundred was a bargain.

These negotiations are typically quite intense, even though the bride does not actually receive the money during the marriage. Instead, she receives it if the marriage ends in divorce. It is your alimony. The bride's family usually negotiates for more, while the groom's is determined to give less. The outcome is written into the marriage contract. Our plan was to go behind my family's back and cancel the agreement immediately afterward the marriage contract was signed. To me it was no big deal, but to him it was. Although I was quite flippant about it, I now realize that those six hundred coins are worth millions of Canadian dollars.

Several times after we married, Bahador said, "I thought you said you would cancel it," to which I replied, "What are you afraid of?"

I did not think much about it but Bahador nagged me for five years. Finally, I went with him to have the *merieh* removed from the marriage contract. I felt ashamed that I had lied to my family.

I knew my mother would not allow me to do this. This is why I avoided Bahador's persistent calls to have it cancelled. None of my family knew I cancelled this traditional agreement. I thought we would be together forever. However, I suspected that were we to divorce, Bahador would use his skills as a lawyer to prevent paying the *merieh* anyway. There were plenty of hints that his family's cheapness rubbed off on him. At Bahador's urging, I went to a lawyer and agreed that if we divorce, he will not have to give me anything.

The bride's family is to provide the money for the couple's appliances and furniture. My burly uncles accompanied me on several shopping trips to purchase the *jahiziyeh*, or dowry. Tradition states that my mother should have done this with me, but she was not interested. Bahador, Uncle Sohrab, and I spent days buying all kinds of electronic goods: a Cuisinart mixing bowl; Hoover vacuum cleaner; food processor; bed; toaster; new fridge; washing machine; and dryer. We bought ceramics for entertaining people who Bahador would bring home for dinner.

In the city, and in traditional families, a day is set aside for the entire extended family to come over and admire the *jahziyeh*. Although Bahador's mother wanted us to do this, I put my foot down. No way was I allowing them to traipse through our new home to snoop and judge our belongings in that way.

The one thing we did not purchase, to the horror of my mother-in-law, was a sufficient number of mattresses. Most families have a closet full of mattresses that are used when company arrives. "What are you going to do when you have visitors?" she asked with wide eyes.

Our flat was in the same building as theirs. We were just one floor beneath them. "Sara. If my family were to come and you could not let them stay here, that would be impolite and very bad."

Chapter Six

Visitors could obviously stay with you, I thought, although I could see this answer would destroy our relationship. I could think of nothing to say; I was surprised that this mattered to her. I wanted a little more space between us and my in-laws, but that was not to be.

"My beautiful bride," Bahador's father said after he heard of my request to consider other apartments, "why would you pay rent when you have a place of your own here? Live here for a year and if anyone bothers you, then you'll be free to leave." I accepted this because I did not want to be one of those bad brides who separates her husband from his family.

On the first day of the Persian New Year, Bahador and I visited my mother. It is custom to visit your parents and older relatives on this day. When we returned home, I opened our door and heard someone inside. I panicked, worried that a thief had broken in. Instead, there was my mother-in-law. She let herself in while we were out.

The way I looked at her made her say, "Am I not allowed to come into my son's home?"

I was confused. Earlier that day, I had phoned her to wish her a Happy New Year. She had not mentioned that she was in our home. I was angry but tried not to show it. She stayed with us for a week in order to avoid a fight with her younger son who lived upstairs in their home.

My inability to hide the fact that I did not appreciate her barging into our home, uninvited, was only one of the things she was upset about. There was always something she did not approve of. I was too modern, she implied, which is a euphemism for not moral enough. Soon, however, she would have a bigger battle to fight with me. She discovered our dream to move to Canada and she was worried that I would take her son away from her.

At first, she was impressed with the idea of her son having a Canadian passport. However, it is when she heard that we prepared our paperwork and that officials were processing our application, that the dramatics started. Once the realization sunk in, she collapsed in a heap on the floor, wailing that she could not survive without her eldest son.

Chapter Seven

"It's never easy to leave one's home,

*especially when there are only
closed doors ahead of you."*

~ Nadia Hashimi

Little Sara of Tehran

It is March 12, 2007. My husband and I have landed in Calgary, Alberta, Canada, where Sayeh lives with her husband. This time it is more than just a tourist visit. I am so excited I can hardly contain myself.

"Where are you coming from?" the custom officer asks.

There is not a hint of friendliness. He speaks crisply and quickly. I feel giddy as I look at him, while he remains stern, looking only at our passports and other documents. I want him to see my enthusiasm, for him and the other officials to show they are aware of all it takes for people to do what Bahador and I have achieved. I have been working to be allowed to make Canada our home for a full seven years. SEVEN YEARS. I have been collecting documents and having them stamped to prove that we are who our documents say we are, going to interviews at the Canadian embassy in Istanbul, and waiting so long between each part of the application process. This is the final step: using the paperwork to see if it works. Will these golden documents open the gates to the new life I have dreamed of?

I am so happy today and I am feeling girlish, and so playful that I imagine myself ducking down lower to catch those eyes that peer downwards at our papers. I try to dampen my feeling of euphoria, to understand he is just doing his job. He has to be serious in case people have dead bodies in their luggage . . . or in our cases, an explosive, as I consider the international reputation of Middle Eastern people in Western media. Even this concerning stereotype does little to sober my happiness. My happiness is so physical that I feel drunk. My attempt to look and act more serious lasts all of two seconds.

"Iran," I reply and something in my voice makes him look up. My smile naturally widens. I am hoping he will realize I am not a terrorist or anyone to be mistrusted. I am a woman whose

Chapter Seven

dreams are finally coming true. He looks down again, examining the immigration cards that I carefully completed for both Bahador and myself.

"What did you bring with you?"

C'mon, I think. What a ridiculous question. I wish now I had brought balloons and confetti and a big "I did it—I'm in Canada" sign. Can he not see how proud and excited I am? Despite coming off a twenty-hour flight I am energized. I want him to ask me something more relevant, something like: "Do you have anything with you that should make us doubt our faith that you will make this country an even better place to live?" To which I'd reply, "I am over the moon and just want to dive into my sister's arms and give her a big hug. Thank you, I will forever remember this moment and look forward to contributing to society here. It is safe for you to let me into Canada, suitcases and all."

He looks up and waits. My smile wanes a bit.

"Our luggage has clothing and some personal stuff," I reply. I am fidgeting like a child who is the next in line to get on a pony ride. I realize that the fidgeting might make me look like I am lying. I stop. I feel the furrows form on my forehead. Involuntarily, my hand reaches for my forehead to control my thoughts. This makes me smile again at the humanity of it all.

"Are you carrying more than ten thousand dollars in cash?" he asks.

I want to dramatically cast my arm behind me and make an announcement on behalf of myself and the other immigrants lined up behind me. For all us I would say, "Listen, we are finally here, in the land of freedom and opportunities. It took me many years to get these papers which say I am now a permanent resident of Canada. You are not asking the right questions. Ask us what we hope for then let us through and into your country, so we can start creating our Canadian lives."

He looks at my passport and papers, not into my eyes.

I say, "No, we are not."

"What do you do for a living?"

"I'm a medical laboratory technologist," I reply confidently. "My husband is a lawyer."

He flicks through the passport and papers, examining each curve of each letter on the papers as I consider his question far more deeply than he intended. Oh, Canada. If only I had been born and raised here. I would not have been a medical laboratory technologist, that I know for sure. If I had been born here, what would I have become? I was always good at physical education, English, and literature. Out of all my classes, I loved these subjects most, more than the science I studied to become a medical technologist. I won a medal in gymnastics when I was eight. I was tiny and powerful. My coach told my mom to allow me to be trained in Russia as he felt I had the talent to become the second Nadia Comaneci. My parents refused as it would have compromised my education. That was the end of my gymnastic days. Perhaps I would have become a gymnast if I had been born here. Would I have become a pianist?

"Are you shipping anything to Canada?"

"Sorry, could you say that to me again, please?" I ask.

I am having a bit of trouble understanding his English. It's faster, more staccato, than what I have heard before. I did not make out what he said quickly enough.

He stares at me and waits with unblinking intensity. He

Chapter Seven

starts to repeat himself speaking slower this time, and without taking his eyes off mine, like he is a human lie detector. I suddenly comprehend and reply, interrupting him mid-sentence: "Shipping? Oh no!" I roll my eyes and smile. "I am not shipping anything."

I wonder if he thinks that I am like all the Iranians who move to Canada and ship their Persian carpets, ornate furniture, and silver cutlery. I want him to understand that I am not traditional. This is one way I may not be like those who are lined up behind me. I am ready to be Canadian and buy Canadian carpets, furniture, and cutlery.

"We are only going to stay here for a month," I say. I am hiding the disappointment in my own heart as I admit this. My husband thinks he needs to save more money in order for us to move to Canada permanently. This, in part, had to do with the fact that when we bought our tickets, his mother cried for an hour, begging him not to leave her. I want to say, Officer, despite all it took to get all those papers you are flipping through, because of the dramatics of his mother, we are only on vacation. I sigh involuntarily. Then I rephrase and say, "Shipping? Well, maybe. But nothing is arranged for that right now." I am sweating and hoping I will pass the test and the interrogation will stop.

"Welcome to Canada." He stamps our passports and hands them back with the rest of the papers. With a nod of his head, we are through.

The Persian New Year—March 21—is not far away. My mother is also in Calgary. She arrived just before us. I am overjoyed to celebrate the New Year with my mother, my sister, her husband, and mine. Almost all my loved ones are together in Canada.

I have not seen my sister for several years. I spot Sayeh right away. I see no one else. We greet each other in a loud, messy, emotional, Persian way. I rush through the frosted glass doors as soon as they open, leaving Bahador to manage our trolleys, piled high with suitcases. We scream as we run towards each other. Behind her are throngs of people also waiting to collect their loved ones. Finally, I can release my joy and I feel it all around me; the whole airport feels like it is about to erupt in celebration. Our excitement mixes with that of other families as they also reunite with people.

Sayeh quietens and politely hugs Bahador. I am reminded that they do not like each other. I am too happy to let any of that spoil any aspect of this momentous day.

Sayeh does not let go of my arm as we leave the airport. Our husbands follow behind, pushing the trolleys. Her hair is colored black and styled to touch her shoulders. She looks beautiful. We stop in the parking section, waiting for the elevator to take us to their car. Sayeh reaches out to touch my hair and I smile as we both know it is momentous that I am not wearing a hijab. "You haven't had such long hair since you were seventeen. It makes you look so young, Sara."

She speaks Farsi. "English, Sayeh, English! I have to get used to speaking like a Canadian now," The sky is a pure blue, the air is cold and crisp. The white snow makes everything look brighter and fresher. It is almost sparkling. I am in awe of everything that I see through the car windows as we drive from the airport. Sayeh points out local landmarks. I note that the streets are clean, there are no aggressive drivers, scarves, or Morality Police. I feel like I am lighter than the clear, unpolluted air. It is Sayeh's voice that keeps me grounded and connected to the real world. We have actually done it. We were now permanent residents of Canada. We now have choices open to us.

Sayeh and her husband live in a beautiful house in the

Chapter Seven

suburbs. I wonder if Bahador and I will live in our own house in the suburbs. I dream of living in Toronto. Although Sayeh and I are not as close as we had been as teenagers, it feels so good to be with her now. Perhaps we should stay in Calgary and grow closer.

The next day, we all go out for lunch at a restaurant in a large mall. Everything about Canada seems huge. There are large department stores that are several stories high. I am curious and check out row upon row of different varieties of the same things. I try to look normal.

A white woman whisks by carrying several shopping bags and I can smell the familiar scent of a Chanel perfume that my mother wears. Ahead of me, an Asian woman pushes a baby buggy. She looks back and I see her wait for her husband who is coaxing a boy— who looks to be about five— from a toy shop's window. We approach a kiosk and the two men working appear to be Persian. As I pass them, I strain to hear them speak and wonder if their accents match mine. I smile as I hear English spoken all around me. I have only a bit of trouble understanding the language.

This is a new world where I can finally be free. I grab Bahador's hand. This is what I have always imagined for myself. No one is wearing a hijab and to me, everything looks relaxed and normal. I am normal.

"It's never busy like the markets back home, here. Even on a Saturday," says Sayeh. She knows how I feel. She knows how different this society is to the one we grew up in. I have always wanted to walk outside on the street without worrying about fixing my hijab or covering my hair. I have wanted to breathe fresh air and experience equality. Three teenage girls pass, they giggle and despite the cold outside, in this mall, they have removed their coats. They wear tight jeans, their tops cropped, revealing their innocent tummies. Two of the girls are white, one I assume to be of Indian background. Behind them are boys rushing to catch up to them. So normal. I am grateful to be in a peaceful country that has not experienced a recent revolution, war, or any other major armed conflict.

The following week, Bahador suggests that we rent a car and drive to Vancouver, British Columbia. I could not be happier. It will be nice to get some time alone. We choose a blue Toyota Yaris and map our route. It will take over ten hours, but we are in no rush. We opt to take the longer route to take in the beautiful scenery along the way. We take frequent breaks, stopping in the Rockies, Banff, and Lake Louise. The views are breathtaking. We finally stop at a small hotel in Kamloops, BC. I feel like life is beyond my dream come true.

I watch Bahador as he drives us. I mentally trace his profile. This is the man I love. We are driving across Canada together, free, married, in love. Although I know that my desire to move here is stronger than his, I know he is here for me and also happy to be in Canada.

Later, we check into the Holiday Inn in Vancouver. The view from our room on the top floor is spectacular. We decide to go to the hotel's restaurant for a nice dinner and later to return to our room for an early night. I feel connected to Bahador. He shares my dream of a life without turmoil. He is a successful lawyer in Tehran, and I know it is a big leap of faith to recreate our careers here, but we have decided to do it together.

I want to stay in Canada from this day onward but my beloved Bahador repeats that we will go back home and save more money in order to build our life here. I see his point and the wisdom of his plan. I believe him. I no longer feel like he is dragging his feet or doing this to please his mother.

Chapter Seven

We unpack our bags and get ready for bed. He is wearing only pajama bottoms and I admire his hairy chest. I put on a negligee that I know he likes. He turns on the TV and finds the news.

"You know, babe," I say while lying down next to him. "Maybe we should start thinking about having a baby. It's been seven year since we were married." I snuggle into him. My head rests on his chest as he strokes my hair with his free hand, the other is holding the TV remote. I feel his stomach muscles constrict.

"We still need to work out our problems before we think about having kids," he says, shifting his body so that I must also move. He flips through the channels as I prop myself up on the many soft pillows on the bed. I do not say anything. My eyes feel as though they are popping out of my face, like a cartoon character.

We still need to work out our problems. What problems is he referring to? We have small disagreements here and there, like any couple, but we never fight. Plus, his parents have been after us to have children since the day after our marriage. I know how happy a grandchild would make them.

This resistance to having children seems suspicious. He is Persian. Family is important to Persians, especially married ones. I wonder why he hasn't been pressuring me to have a baby, why is he firmly rejecting this idea now. I suddenly feel cold. I shiver and say nothing.

I pull the blankets up over me and stare at the TV screen. I cannot hear or understand a word they are saying. My brain will not process it. All I hear is that sentence: "We still need to work out our problems." I am in a strange city, in a strange country, with a man I do not understand. As we head back to Calgary, I pretend that everything is okay but inside my head, I re-examine every word of every conversation I can remember. What am I missing?

We arrive at my sister's house and I am both afraid to yet also desperate to talk to my mother alone. The next morning, I am sitting with Maman, when my sister rushes in with the phone. She is furious. She holds her hand over the mouthpiece and mouths to us, "Listen to this!" She holds the receiver over my ear, still holding her hand over the mouthpiece. I recognize my husband's voice. He is speaking in an intimate tone to Rina, his secretary. She tells him she misses him. I take the phone from Sayeh and we all listen intently.

"I will be back soon," my husband says followed by what my sister later insisted was a kissing sound. My whole world collapses in that instant. Sayeh takes the phone from me. She knows that in the blindness of my anger, I might throw it through her window.

I walk upstairs. My heart pounds. My temples feel like the blood might explode as it pulses into my brain. I am in a fog.

"Who were you just speaking with?" I ask. I wait for him to tell the truth.

"My mother," he answers.

Something inside of me snaps. "How is this even possible?" I am screaming with every breath in my lungs, with every muscle in my body. "How could you? We're happy! I thought we were happy! I thought you loved me! How could you? How stupid am I?"

I scream and sob. I lunge towards him, but my sister runs in and pulls me away. Then I collapse into a fetal position on the floor. I scream at him, reminding him of all the things I have done for him.

"So, this is the problem we need to work out? Go back to Iran and never call me again. I hate you and myself for being so stupid. For trusting you and making you my priority in life."

Chapter Seven

That night, I kicked him out. He cried and tried to tell me I was wrong. For the first time, I did not care about him. I was focused on my pain. I made him leave my sister's house in the middle of winter. I did not care that he did not speak English well or that he did not know the city or the country.

I am surprised that I did not have a heart attack. I had never experienced emotions that strong in my life. I had never exploded like that. The next morning, I feel small and drained. I am embarrassed that my mother, my sister, and my brother-in-law witnessed this. My throat is raw from the screaming, my eyes are red, and my skin is blotchy. I feel betrayed. I truly thought we were the perfect couple.

How stupid I am, I say to myself on loop and it feels like the loop will never stop.

Clearly, I had somehow forgotten myself in order to become the woman I thought he wanted me to be but apparently, that was not enough. I was not enough.

I spent my life running from the feeling that I was not enough. Before getting engaged, my husband and I dated for three years, which my culture considered too long for a courtship. I waited for Bahador as he finished his master's degrees. I supported him while putting my own life on hold. I idolized my husband. I loved him dearly and did everything in my power to keep him happy: from putting a delicious dinner on the table every evening, to keeping the house clean and comfortable every day.

Considering how unhappy my parent's marriage was because my father would not let my mother work, plus, the experience of living through their two divorces and arguments, I did everything I thought a good wife should do. I allowed my husband to dictate my career. And although this did not sit well with me at times,

I still did what he wanted even when it contrasted with my own desires. As I lay, feeling horrible about my life that was in pieces around me, I remembered an out-of-character discussion I had with my father soon after I completed my degree. Surprisingly he had advised me to "make sure to have your own career and independence, that way you'll always have power and choice." But I had not and Maman had warned me that his family was more traditional than they appeared. She told me that I would never be happy. I thought of that now, too.

"Can you believe I make *kotlet* at least once a week for him?" I wailed to my mother and sister, who sat with me as I sobbed my heart out, "And it's still not enough?"

Kotlet is lamb. It is Bahador's favorite. I said to him and laughed, "the only way you'd leave me is if you were having a love affair with an actual lamb, so I am making this for you to keep you!"

Making *kotlet* was a big process. Bahador did not let me do the meat shopping myself. Instead, he insisted on buying the meat from the best butcher in the city. Once home, he took his sweet time chopping it up into different sizes and dimensions for different meals. My job was to bag it up all the different packages and freeze them.

On cooking days, I defrosted some of the packages, and got my hands dirty by mixing the ground lamb, eggs, grated onions, and potatoes in a big bowl until it formed a smoothen paste. It was a good workout for the arms. I made it exactly the way his mom did. This meant that I boiled the potatoes, let them cool, then peeled and coarsely grated them. As for the eggs, only the yolk would get in the bowl. I made sure the minced onions were nicely sieved so they had no moisture, otherwise, the mixture would not bind firmly, and they would not come out perfectly.

Chapter Seven

I carefully flattened the paste into oval patties, fried them in oil, and browned them on both sides. I was always careful not to burn them. I garnished the kotlet and served them with a *shirazi* salad. I meticulously diced tomatoes, onions, and cucumber into one-inch cubes (Bahador did not like bigger cubes) and mixed them with lime, fresh parsley, cilantro, and mint.

Looking back, I performed these precise and time-consuming cooking processes every single day with contentment and pride. Not only did I prepare a delicious breakfast and dinner, I also made sure to leave work each afternoon to provide my husband with an elaborate lunch, too. Following this, I cleaned up each mess and ensured no grease marred the surface of the stove. In return, my husband allowed me to work. But only part-time so as to not take away from any spare time he wanted to spend with me

Everything that once felt wonderful had changed almost instantly. I could not speak to Bahador and I did not allow him to even visit my sister's home. I felt lost, alone, hurt, betrayed, and confused. Our one-month visit was up, and I was meant to go back to Iran. But I did not. Bahador returned to Iran without me and from there he did everything he could to win me over. He fired the secretary, and he signed over his law office to me as a way of apologizing and proving his love. I knew how much he loved money. When he gave me power over the business, he had worked so hard to build up, I thought that it must be a sign of his true love.

But I was not able to stop my feelings. I was crushed by his betrayal. The strength of my anger towards him and the red-hot fire of hatred I felt made me want nothing else but to be free of him, but I tried to be rational. I was afraid of making a mistake in that moment that I would come to regret. I thought about all the years I had invested in our relationship, going over every aspect of our lives together. But I could not stay in my head and be only intellectual about this. My heart was broken. How could I have been so wrong? I wondered if it was ever real and if he had ever truly loved me. I did not know what to do. How could the person who had developed a relationship with his secretary be the same one who kissed me under the magnolia tree in Daryenkenar? And why was he fighting for me now?

My mother never gloated or said, "I told you so." She observed our differences from the outset, yet she never even gave me a look that suggested anything other than concern for me. I knew she would support me whether I chose to stay or leave. I decided to be still, to listen to my head and my heart and do what felt right to me. Eventually, I went back to him. I wanted us to work things out. I decided if I was not sure what to do, it must mean that beneath the betrayal, my love for him and our past together was a strong enough foundation. I would go back to him, but my attitude about marriage and pushing down my needs and wants could not continue. I would go back and we would build a stronger, more equal and closer relationship. Our relationship would have to change for it to survive.

***

I spent years trying to save our marriage. I wanted us to try therapy. Unsurprisingly, Bahador did not come with me. It is shameful for a Persian man to seek help. Afterall, he saw himself as perfect. *Doodool talah*. From his perspective, he knew everything. Therefore, surely a problem could not lie with him. His mother asked what I had done to make her son look for another woman.

Two years after our near break up, I got pregnant. The pregnancy was unplanned; I did not want to have the baby. However, Bahador and I were married, and the decision was not mine to make alone. "For god's sake!" I implored during one of our discussions. "We're moving to a new country in a few months.

Chapter Seven

We don't have jobs and don't know if we can survive. Let's not complicate this more."

I was heartbroken, but sure of my decision. I knew, in my heart, that he would not let me leave the country with a child and it was increasingly clear that his desire to move to Canada was not as strong as mine. I would stay in the marriage because of the baby. I expected him to fight me, leveraging a baby to keep me tied down. To my surprise, he agreed to the abortion. Coming from a traditional man, this was confirmation to me that our broken relationship was irreparable. Still, I was not yet ready to walk away from it.

In July 2009, we returned to Canada. This time, permanently. Or so I thought. We purchased a small condo in Toronto for our anniversary in the hopes that we could build something new and fresh. Bahador leased a top-of-the-line white BMW and bragged to his family and friends about the "gift" he got for me. One day, as I ordered lunch for us in English at our new favorite restaurant, he admitted that he was struggling with the language. I could see that he was frustrated, but I felt he was not trying hard enough. He made little effort to practice.

"If I could speak English as well as you, I would own Canada by now," he said.

A statement like that would have made me mushy inside a couple of years ago, but now I saw the grandiosity in him that I had mistaken for confidence. His arrogance meant he was not willing to be vulnerable enough to accept his English was not perfect and to work hard enough to improve it. He had to feel as though he was the smartest person in the room, or his ego would be crushed.

Despite his promise to stay in Canada, it became obvious that he was not willing to leave his family or his career behind for a new life. He was only interested in the prestige of Canadian citizenship and vacationing here once in a while and the truth is, at this point, I knew I did not even want him to stay. I had changed too much and was no longer willing to compromise myself. The differences between us— that I had once been blind to— were all too clear. Yet, I flew back to Iran with him after this short visit to Canada. I did not know how to leave the marriage. I was plagued with doubts, scared I would regret ending things.

My mom knew that I was not happy. She could see I was confused, lost, and frustrated with my life. "Sara," she said, as we shared coffee together. We sat on her red velvet couch in the small apartment she moved into after Baba died. "You can't bounce back and forth between Iran and Canada, vacationing here and there. You worked hard to get this Permanent Resident card and make your dream come true. I know you're still doing this to save your marriage and your relationship. But you will never know if you really want to live in Canada unless you get a job there and experience the authentic way of living in a new country. If your marriage is meant to last, it can survive this."

It is now 2010. I decided to return to Toronto with the intention of settling down, getting a job, and making it my new home. Bahador did not protest. Once I arrived, I did some volunteer work at the local YMCA. Landing in a new country is one thing. Landing a job and fitting in is a different story. I believed that a university degree, work experience, and money in the bank would help, but I soon realized that it was not enough. I accepted the challenge to start from scratch.

As I was starting from scratch, I decided to switch careers. I wanted to teach. When I told Sayeh, she disagreed and begged me to look for a job in the medical technology field. "You're making a big mistake, Sara," she told me. "You don't have a chance at getting hired. They are going to hire native speakers, plus, teaching English does not pay well. This is not Iran."

Despite her well-intentioned advice, I knew in my gut that teaching was for me. Sayeh had a point though. She knew the system better and she was my older sister. I had grown up looking up to her and taking her advice. I respected her as a strong woman and did not want to disappoint her. Courageously, I took a chance. I obtained my Teaching English as a Second Language (TESL) training certificate and applied for a job at a private college. Within a week, I heard back. I got the job.

Persians always complain about difficulty finding the jobs they want here. I wondered how this happened for me so easily. Perhaps it was the power of positivity and mindset, a practice I still continued with my mother even though she was no longer directly involved with Pana. I picked up the phone and called her, despite the time difference. It was midnight there.

"Maman, did I wake you up?"

"No dear. I was reading. Are you alright?" As usual, her voice was calm and kind. I felt her care through the phone.

"Guess what? I got the job! I got the job! I start on Monday!" I cried of happiness.

She cried too. "I knew you would. I had no doubt. You are my beautiful smart girl. You can do whatever you put your mind into. Congratulations, my baby."

There it was: a new beginning for me. My next call was to Bahador. I asked if he was willing to move to Toronto and start afresh. He was not interested. For him, Canada was not the land of opportunity. He would have to leave behind a successful law firm, not to mention his family. He suggested that I live and work in Canada while he traveled back and forth from Iran. Six months here, six months there. But I knew, in my heart, that it was over anyway. I wanted a divorce.

Once I made up my mind, that was it. I talked to my mom on the phone the next day. I informed her of my final decision. I knew she was there for me, and she confirmed that I had her support.

I had no idea that I would never hear her voice again.

Chapter Eight

"I learned that every mortal will taste death.

But only some will taste life."

~ Rumi

August 18, 2010 is a gorgeous sunny morning. I have been working at the college teaching English to as a second language for a few weeks now. My students are young adults who have come to Canada specifically to learn the language. I love my emerging life in Toronto. I look out and admire the lakefront view from my eighteenth-floor condo and say to myself, "Is anyone luckier than I am?" I have it all. Everything I envisioned for the past few years has finally manifested.

The view is enviable, there are no buildings obstructing my view of Lake Ontario, Center Island, and the streets below. It is a Toronto scene like no other. People climb on and off the streetcar, others walk on the sidewalk, probably on their way to work. I see joggers, and adults walking their dogs. It's lively and active. I don't feel alone.

I get ready for work, take a shower, put on my makeup, and decide which pair of high heels match my outfit best. High heels are new for me. They are exciting. Perhaps this is because it makes up for all those years that I went to work wearing a *roosari*, a long scarf wrapped as a hijab and only flat shoes. Or perhaps I simply want to feel taller than my four-foot ten frame and chicer in this new city. Persians are known for dressing well and taking care of themselves. In terms of fashion, we are more European than North American. I am excited to wear heels and color coordinate my work outfits, especially as I always wore black in public when I was back home.

As I drive to work, I listen to a radio show called "The War of the Roses," where the hosts chat with someone who suspects that their partner is cheating. We did not have any reality radio, or TV, shows in Iran. All Iranian programs are censored, which renders shows cliché, and predictable. In Iran, cheating exists, but is certainly not broadcasted on the radio. The same men who

Chapter Eight

pilgrim to Mecca— which is considered to be the House of God— are the ones who return home to flirt and fool around with women who are not their wives.

"You found another woman's underwear at your place?" the host asks the caller.

I am fascinated. It is a true culture shock to hear a woman conspire with a radio host to catch her boyfriend cheating. I am absorbed in the show, as I watch out for cyclists and cars stopping in typically slow Toronto traffic. I wonder how these women could not see what jerks their boyfriends are. But I am in no position to judge. This is all too familiar to me. I myself could not shake my suspicions after that disastrous discovery on the phone at my sister's house. To this day, I am unsure if his affair was something serious, or it was just a stupid flirtation, like my uncles suggested. I liked to believe that they did not sleep with each other. But we all want to believe what we want to believe. In this show, the caller does get the full truth. In the grand scheme of things, the truth matters less than the permanent mistrust created. I laugh at how serious and philosophical I am being.

At 8:00am, the news starts. Halfway through my commute, the phone rings. I lower the volume on the radio, expecting to hear my mom's lovely voice. It was not unusual for her to surprise me with an early morning call. I smile when I accept the call but it is not my mother. It is my uncle.

"Hi Sara, where are you?" my uncle Sohrab asks.

"I'm wonderful! I'm driving to work. What's new?" I say. He never calls me, but I figure he must be calling to report that someone is getting married or some other similarly big news.

"Sara, your mother is in the hospital, in the Critical Care Unit, the CCU. The doctors told us to call her daughters to come back home." There is a long, long silence as I continue to drive.

My heart stops beating and my stomach sinks. What is he talking about? I spoke to her two days ago and she was fine. The feelings of lightness I started the day with abruptly come to an end, like a car skidding to a stop. I start crying and cannot stop. Everything is blurry and hazy. I manage to get to work, but I am weeping and shaking. I try to bypass my colleagues. I tell myself, "You can't cry here, Sara. This is Canada, it is different from Iran. People don't show emotions in public. Keep it together."

I wipe my face and I use all the strength I have to hold back my tears. It is obvious I am upset but I do my best to be calm. I sit at a desk in a room with several others and no privacy. I cannot concentrate as it all feels unreal. I go out through the emergency exit in order to compose myself.

I call Shahin. I am closest to him. My husband answers the phone. What is he doing there?

"Alo, Sara." Bahador's voice is shaky.

My heart stops again. I can barely hear my own voice as I struggle to ask the question they have not answered. It is unrecognizable to me. I force sound out, as if my throat were a constricted tunnel. "Is she alive?" I have a sinking feeling that she's gone, but am desperate to hear someone say, "She's sick and she needs you to come right away, but she'll be okay. Just come home. She is waiting for you!"

Bahador does not say a word. I can hear him cry, then I hear the voice of Shahin.

I try again. "Shahin, please tell me the truth. Is my mom…" I pause, "alive?" I hear my own heart beating, hoping to hear a "yes", but somehow, I know I will not.

Chapter Eight

Shahin bursts into tears. I can hardly hear what he is saying. "Your mom is gone, Sara. My beloved sister is gone."

It is like someone has pulled the rug from under my feet. I truly understand that expression now. My world collapses for the second time. I am dizzy and need to get to my desk, grab my purse and keys, and then get to Iran. I sob as I leave the stairwell. I cannot stand, so I lean on colleagues who rush to me. They usher me to an enclosed space. They want to give me privacy from my students. They speak to me in soft tones and each of them gives me a North American hug, which is different from the warm, tight hugs of the Middle East. I am desperate for support and comfort during one of the worst moments of my life. I tell my boss that I will need to go home to Iran and that I am unsure when I will return. I cannot think clearly. My mom has died, and I was not there.

The tears I shed are different from all tears I have shed in the past. I no longer have any living parents. I consider my life. My sister does not understand me. I have left my husband. I sit in disbelief for the entire twenty-hour flight to Tehran. A big group of family and friends, including Shahin and my husband, are waiting for me at the airport. They drive me to my mom's apartment. It is in a busy neighborhood in the city yet has a beautiful view of the mountain. "I like to see the mountains and people buzzing around. I won't feel alone." She said when I suggested the area might be a bit too loud.

Now, more than ever, I know how my mother must have felt.

Shahin opens the door. The house is dead, too. My mom is not there to open the door with her big smile or hug me with her soft chubby arms. It is disarming. I can hear her voice calling my name, asking me what I am hungry for so she can prepare it for me. I pick up her *sepas,* her gratitude notebook, and take it into the bedroom with me.

Her most recent entry was, "Dear God, today I'm grateful for my beautiful daughters who treat me with love and respect. I'm grateful for Sara and her positive attitude and for her caring nature towards me. I'm grateful for this beautiful sunshine and the birds' chirping. I'm grateful for my work for life and being alive…I feel lonely though." The entry went on and on for a few pages. I cry and cry. Eventually, I cry myself to sleep.

It is a hot day, and despite it being nearly ten degrees warmer than Toronto, it is comfortable. I prefer the dry heat of Tehran to the heavy humidity of Toronto. I wear all black, including a hijab as we head to Behesht e Zahra, the main cemetery of Tehran. It is one of the largest cemeteries in the world and is always busy. All I see around me are people in black and all I hear are cries and the sound of Azan, the Muslims' ritual prayer. I feel like the loneliest person in the world. This is the same cemetery where we buried my dad. I am haunted by the brutality and finality of death.

When my father was dying, we watched him diminish daily over a span of five years. He lost weight and strength. When he died, we were relieved to see the end of his suffering. His body was wrapped in a simple white cloth and we watched as he was laid in a deep grave. In Muslim funerals, bodies are buried without being placed in a wood casket of any sort. They are laid in the grave in a *kafan*, a thin cotton sheet. On the day of his burial, one of my uncle's close friends jumped in with him. From above the ground, I could hear him reciting prayers from the Quran.

"What the heck is he doing?" I asked Shahin.

"He's insinuating that he's dead," he replied, an answer that made no more sense than what I was hearing.

"Go closer, Sara. Go and say goodbye to your dad."

I was exhausted and devastated. I reluctantly did what

Chapter Eight

Shahin instructed. I stepped closer to the grave and peered in. I witnessed the most horrifying scene and it has been engraved in my brain ever since. When I think of my father, that image comes to me as strongly as the many loving ones. My beloved father's soulless, skinny face had been exposed, the *kafan* was pulled away. My uncle's friend shook his body, as if he were a piece of meat. I could hardly breathe. I grew nauseous and felt bile rise up to my throat. The sight broke me into pieces. Weeping over my dad's grave, I held my mother's hand with one hand, and Bahador's with the other. "Your dad is in a better place now. He's not suffering anymore." That was all Shahin could say to comfort me.

Now I stand by the mortuary where my mother's body is being washed. I am determined not to relive a violent burial experience. I do not want to see my mother's lifeless body. She was cuddly, warm, and full of life when I last saw her. She died so suddenly, the autopsy revealed, due to a heart aneurysm. There were no warning signs. She certainly never complained of anything when I spoke with her.

"Don't you want to look at your mom to say goodbye?" asked an elderly friend of the family. In a Muslim funeral service, there is no viewing. However, I had the option to look through a window as she was washed before being wrapped in the *kafan* for burial.

"No," I say. "I want to remember my mom's beautiful face as it was. I saw my dad's face after his death, and it was enough."

"Well, you *should* look," she says, pointing to the window, "if you want to believe she is dead."

Why do religious people always make things complicated?

Suddenly, this old woman grabs me around the hips and takes a few steps towards the window, lifting me up. I was too short to see through the window from the ground, which I had considered a blessing. Although I struggle against her surprising strength, I look through the window and I see a heart-wrenching view that I will never forget. There lies my mother, swollen and purple. She wears the most beautiful smile. I let out an agonized scream of shock and despair. It is real. She is gone forever.

***

Three weeks after the funeral, I return to Toronto only to discover that my teaching position had been filled. I am numb. Bahador is with me. He visits for a week, hoping to take me back home with him. He does all he can to stop me from filing for divorce.

"You cannot do this at this time, Sara. Who would go through two major losses at the same time?"

Despite his being there for me during my stay in Iran, much of my anger is directed at him. I recalled his disparaging comments about my mother, here and there. I am still confused. It would be much easier for me to return to Iran. After losing my mother, I did not care if he was seeing someone else. If I stay married and remain in Canada, he would continue to send me money from Iran to pay my mortgage as well as the lease on the BMW, which he told everyone he bought me for our anniversary. Like so many other couples, we could live a double life.

But I decide otherwise, and know that staying with him, whether in Iran or Canada, is not for me. Not even now, when I am vulnerable and need someone to take care of me. Instead, I choose to continue on my path and tell my husband to go home. And to show him I was serious, I annulled the power of attorney he had given me over his law office. I turn my back on all the wasted energy I have spent hating him. I see the true reason for this period, for losing so much and being stuck, as if rock bottom is made of iron and I am a magnet. I am stuck to the horror of losses and struggle to even lift my head. I see I was upset with the wrong being. It was not all due to Bahador. It was God.

God is trying to teach me a lesson.

Every night I cry, praying for God to show me a way. I call out to my mother and my father, begging them to come to me in my dreams and tell me what to do. I question why I am still in Canada. Everything has turned upside down, just like in a fantasy movie where a witch shakes up the world and everything good dies with the mere flick of her wand. Yet, something inside me strengthens whenever I think of my mom. I cannot stop thinking of our last conversation and the advice she gave me the last time we spoke. That night I dream of her and I hear her say what I need to hear, and this keeps me going. A voice in my head, her voice, says "Try living in Canada. Get settled, get a job and make friends. If you're not happy, go back to Iran. At least you'd have tried."

Chapter Nine

"Dance, when you're broken open. Dance, if you've torn the bandage off. Dance in the middle of the fighting. Dance in your blood. Dance when you're perfectly free."

~ *Rumi*

"She's a strong, tough girl, Safieh," said my grandmother to my mother. From the time I was just two years old, my grandmother recognized this in me. "She'll be able to knock a man off his horse if she needs to."

My grandmother raised seven children: my mother and her six brothers. Who would know strength and grit better than her? But I felt I had lost these qualities. In my despair, I appeal to my dead mother and grandmother. I ask them, "If I could knock someone off a horse, how come I feel so powerless right now? How come I don't know what I want anymore? How come I feel so lonely and so helpless?"

It is the winter of 2010 and I am thirty-five years old. I need my recently deceased mother. My sister and I have grown even more distant since her death. I now resent her attempts to guide me. They are not what I need. I need her to listen and remind me that I can do anything I am determined to do; I am feeling so down that I need her to motivate me just like our mother used to. Instead, she offers only cautious advice which makes the chasm between us greater and makes me yearn for Maman. I would give anything to hear Maman say, "elahi ghorboone oon soorate mahet beram man,"—*I love your beautiful face*—just one more time. I would die to hear her say those words, which she said so often when she was alive. Such a simple request and so few words, but this one thing I yearn for not even God can deliver to me.

I feel empty. With further reflection, I wonder if finding a man to love me would make the emptiness go away. Or perhaps going back to school for a master's degree will keep me busy and distracted. But I love my students at the ESL school where I still teach. Perhaps opening my own ESL school will fill the void? After all, I have always wanted to have my own business.

The emptiness follows me everywhere whether I am at home

Chapter Nine

eating dinner on my own, in bed waiting for sleep to take me, out shopping, or in front of my beloved students. I am finally living in the land of freedom and opportunity. I have no one to answer to. It's just me, myself, and I. It's everything I was dreaming of. The reality of it feels scary and has no value for me anymore. I have it all. Now what?

For the first time, my confidence deserts me. It is like a slow leak that I at first do not notice until I start criticizing myself about things that never bothered me before. I feel small. My height never bothered me when I was in Iran, but here I am noticeably shorter than most people. I stand at only four feet ten inches and a new awareness of this difference seeps in and infects the way I see myself. It makes me feel small: figuratively and literally. In Canada, I must always hem the pants that I purchase in stores. When I visit the bank, I usually stand on my tiptoes when I am behind a counter. At home, I sit on a chair with my legs crossed but if I am at someone's home, and the sofa is deep, then I make sure to sit on the edge or put a cushion behind me so my feet do not dangle.

"Wow! How tall—or rather small—are you, Sara?"

"Why are you so short?"

"Hey, shorty!"

"You could get away with buying the kids' ticket! Hahaha"

"What do you eat over there? Is it something you guys eat that has stunted your growth?"

I hear these comments, yet I would have laughed them off before. I have become conscious and focused on my height. I am used to sarcasm and jokes in Iran. Here, I am not always sure how to respond. People in Canada have asked me how I can drive my big SUV. What a silly question, I think to myself. The seats are adjustable. I was asked these questions back home too. But it feels different here. Before, I did not feel any wounds from innocently made comments. Here, I take all comments, even when it is clear they were made as jokes, and I analyze them and often turn them against myself, using the comments as further proof that I cannot fix things. I am vulnerable from my loss and my lack of direction in life.

My anger and vulnerability drive me to do risky things which sabotage myself. I go ice-skating with my students. It feels great as I remembered the days I used to skate back home when I was little. I get carried away, speed and have an awful fall.

"Teacher! Teacher! Your head!!" My students are scared. There is a strawberry-size lump on my temporal bone.

"I'm fine, don't worry," I lie with a big smile. I am in so much pain that I cry as I drive myself to the emergency department. I thought I had a concussion as I was becoming dizzy. I didn't but I had broken my wrist. Over the next few weeks, I struggle taking showers and putting on clothes while my arm is in a plaster cast. The black eye, my broken wrist, and my obvious weight loss are worrying my sister. "Come and live with us, Sara!" Sayeh insists.

"No, I'm okay. I was just being a bit too adventurous," I reply.

***

I am approaching the first Christmas since my mother's passing and the separation from my husband. It is also my first Christmas in Canada, and my employer has given us all two weeks off work. Everyone else is spending time with their families. I ask my sister to travel to Mexico with me. "Are you insane? It's dangerous down there! I'm not going, and you shouldn't go either!" she scolds.

Chapter Nine

I ask a couple of the new friends I have made. They also have plans to see their families. I do not want to stay in Toronto alone in my quiet condo with its huge panes of glass windows through which the view gives no comfort. Instead, the view adds to my loneliness by reflecting back the bleak cold of the frozen lake so many feet below. The thought of two weeks of this confinement was impossible to imagine.

Then, I have another dream.

In the dream, I am desolate. I sob to my mom, "no one will go to Mexico with me." My dream-mom smiles that big smile I love and says, "Screw everyone! I'll go with you and we'll have fun!"

I still get goosebumps when I think about that dream.

The next morning, I jump out of bed and go to the first travel agency I can find. I book an all-inclusive package to Mexico. It is my first vacation alone. I have never been on an all-inclusive trip, and I learn that it means that I can eat, drink, party, swim, and relax as much as I want, without breaking any social rules as there are so few.

I arrive in Mexico and stroll around with a drink in hand at all times of the day. There is no shame in this behavior here. Cancun is a city known for its nightlife and entertainment. Although I am separated, grieving, and lonely, I am free. I meet Mina, who is also there on her own, and we become friends. We spend the whole week checking out guys and laughing. Here I am not bound to expectations of what a good girl ought to do.

We dress up and head to CoCo Bongo, a night club featuring dancers and performers who fly over our heads on ropes and wire. I drink two shots of tequila and feel dizzy. Then another two. I have never been big on alcohol. I rush to the bathroom to vomit. To my surprise, the stalls have no doors. I am too drunk to care that others can hear and see me. With my head over the toilet, I curse my ex-husband, while the world spins around my head. I am just like all the other loud people at the pool bars who I would normally have judged as trashy. It is Mina who tells me what I said the next day, and I am shocked when she mentions my husband's name. That night, I took a cab and somehow managed to get to my room safely while the world was spinning around my head. I woke up on the washroom floor and promised myself I would not drink the next day. But I do. The sun warms me, the drunken smiles of strangers seduce me, and the tequila shots numb me.

I flirt with a handsome guy in the lobby. He looks shy but I have a mission: to pick him up. I want to prove to myself that I can have anyone I lay my eyes on. I pick him up and take him to my hotel room.

***

I learned the expression one-night stand from the Oprah show as a girl in Iran. I never thought I'd have one—and I hated myself for doing so. That night is blurry to me now but what is clear is the depth of loneliness I experienced that Christmas

When I returned to Toronto, I needed help to clear my mind. The trip to Mexico was fun, but it increased my feelings of loss. So as suggested by a friend, I did a Landmark Worldwide class. To me, it seemed similar to the work my mother had done with The School of Pana. It was intense, but it opened my eyes and helped me see how I was sabotaging my life. It helped get clarity around my separation. I filed for divorce after I found Landmark, jumped from the plane to prove to myself that I could face my biggest fears, and I ran a successful charity event to raise awareness and money for less fortunate kids in Africa. All this, done through Landmark, helped me boost my confidence.

Chapter Nine

Then I started dating, taking dance classes, and exploring the province. I would do road trips to small towns; I enjoyed the quaint and cute atmosphere of the villages with cobblestoned streets and drove on the frozen Lake Simcoe to an island and had fish and chips at a cozy dinner. While enjoying the view and the experience, the owner mentioned it wasn't safe to drive on the lake at that time of the year. It was March, and he pointed out that things were warming up. But I had to get back the same way I got there. On the whole drive back across the frozen lake, I prayed to God that the ice would not crack and that I would make it back to the shore.

***

Online dating was new to me, but I knew I had to try it as it is how people find partners in Canada. I dated a Persian guy for a little bit. As he had been living in Canada for a long time, I assumed that he would be different from the traditional Persians back home. I ended the burgeoning relationship as soon as I noticed a tiny whiff of *doodool talah*. As soon as I saw a small bit of arrogance and grandiosity in him, I broke up with him. Then I dated an Arab man who sent flowers to my workplace after our first few dates. He showed up at my condo when I told him I was no longer interested in him, yelling, "Tell me to my face if you dare!" After that I decided to forget about the Middle East.

I went on dates with Italian, Russian, and Portuguese men. I assumed that their cultures were similar to mine, but not quite as chauvinistic. I expected these European men to know about Iran and that our shared rich histories would bind us. They did not. Then I found an Irishman. Although his background was Irish, he grew up in North America and like many North Americans, he and his family knew little about Iran. But there was something about him that I really liked, so I ignored that and did what I could to change his toxic views on the country of my blood.

"There are four seasons in Iran," I lectured. "Winter is beautiful and not too cold or too long. I learned how to ski back home. We actually have mountains, not hills! The north of Iran is similar to Vancouver, it is green, and it rains often. The south is hot and humid.

"Yes, women can vote, and they are allowed to drive," I continued, although I doubt that they believed me and probably had stopped listening anyway. "Our Persian Empire goes back 2500 years. Did you know that?

"Iranians are very warm and friendly. We speak Persian not Arabic because we are not Arabs. We have many local and traditional delicious foods. And all of this should tell you, we are not terrorists!"

I figured by getting to know his family, I could change their opinions about the Middle East. This was important as we grew closer and became serious about each other. My desire was that I fit into his family, but this was not easy. I intentionally avoided his dad and brother in-law as they spoke English with a very thick Irish accent.

"Can you tell me what they are talking about?" I whisper to my Irishman. "All I can do is just smile like an idiot."

I was in so much pain trying to fit in.

How am I supposed to have a close relationship with these people when I don't get what they say? I changed myself in order to receive validation from them, proof that I was worth loving, just as I had done with Iman's family and with the family of my ex-husband. When I went to their Christmas parties, and the family talked endlessly about childhood stories, and about movies I had never heard of, I smiled at the appropriate times, without even considering that I was not interested in the slightest. It did not matter that they did not make attempts to know more about me. I wanted to belong, for them to want and love me, at any cost.

We talked about visiting my family and he said, "I've heard they will cut my penis off as soon as I get to the airport in Iran. I am not ready to go," he said. My eyes nearly rolled right out of my head. It was hard for me to believe it, but he was serious. His family seemed kind to me, but despite knowing me, they held onto damaging stereotypes that Iranians are terrorists and live in huts in the desert. His mother warned him against traveling in the Middle East. I could not change their opinion, no matter how much I tried to show them my humanity.

Nonetheless, I loved the Irishman and he and his family grew to love me. His life was far more complicated than mine as although he'd been separated for five years when we met, he was still in the midst of a difficult divorce and a custody battle. He found solace for his grief and guilt over breaking the Catholic rule on divorce though a church in a small-town miles away from Toronto. I worried he was becoming too religious, and I knew what my mother would say if she were here for me to ask. I knew she would say, "he is too traditional, and his focus is not on you, Sara." I went with him to that little church once a month, but I was concerned about having to take a back seat in his life.

When it comes to marriage, Islam demands that my future husband convert to Islam, whereas Catholicism demands that I convert to Catholicism. This was a problem between us. At first, he told me he would be fine if I did not convert to Catholicism. Then he changed his mind. We eventually broke up.

At the same time, I realized that I had to break up with my beloved SUV, too—the one Bahador bragged about to everyone, claiming he'd bought it for me. It was leased, not purchased, and the lease payments were not sustainable with my salary and the diminishing amount of devalued Iranian money I had in a savings account. I knew it was ridiculous to continue paying for it. And I was surprised how difficult it is to give it up. Although I know I'm anonymous in Toronto, and that both the rich and poor rely on public transport here, having the choice removed for me hit me hard. For the first time, I have to budget. People back home would think less of me if they knew I could not afford the finer things. The shame burns me, and I wonder if I can actually make it on my own here. Will I end up crawling back home begging for forgiveness and a place to live while admitting they were right all along?

But I don't go home, of course, I adjust my expenses. I love teaching. Two years into my job, and I finally feel able to handle an ESL class full of students with different linguistic backgrounds. I learn that Japanese students are quite serious. Brazilians and South Americans, on the other hand, want to study and play. Some Saudi Arabian students are here to get away from their strict culture, so they skip classes and rarely listen. At first, I do not know how to manage the classes, keep everyone happy, and be the strict yet fun teacher. I have an unreasonable expectation that all my students have a perfect experience. I crave positive feedback from them.

This expectation, of course, applies to everyone, even those outside of the classroom. I struggle to keep up with English-speakers who talk fast, mumble, or use plenty of slang. I do not allow myself to say "sorry, could you repeat that?" I pressure myself to be perfect at work and perfect when speaking to those outside of work. I am afraid of being judged by others, but I manage to keep the mask on until I get home and am all by myself, I often collapse into bed, drained, exhausted, and too tired to bother with cooking dinner.

Chapter Nine

Back home in Tehran, I did not have to worry about mispronouncing a word or wondering if my last comment come across as stupid or an insulting. I was an educated Persian woman from a respected family. I was someone to be admired. In my first week as a teacher, one of my co-workers asked me, "Where is your accent from?" and I felt she had publicly insulted me. The feeling of shame added to other layers of self-hatred I wore for years as I believed she was being condescending and stating in front of all of our co-workers that I am not as good as her, or the other teachers. That my skills are not enough.

It shocked me two years later to learn that it was just a friendly question, which indicated that she was interested in knowing where I came from. In fact, she *liked* the way my English sounded. I was carrying a crappy attitude with me. I was self-conscious of my English and I did not like when anyone asked me what I did for a living because I felt like an imposter. I was sure I could read their minds and I waited for them to be shocked. I was ready to say: *Yes, I teach English, but I know what you are thinking. You are thinking that my English isn't good enough to teach others and that it is clear I have not got the hang of idioms, expressions, and slang that would make my English sound more natural. Plus, I make grammar mistakes. You and I both know I am not enough.* Yet, I loved teaching and the results showed I was good at it. That question which I had held up as proof I did not belong, was actually an extension of a hand in friendship. How wrong I had been.

Being around my beautiful students, these young souls with their whole lives ahead of them, made me feel younger. They brought out my playful inner child and they never judged me for having an accent. I know their weaknesses and strengths because I shared them. Eventually I was able to mean it when I told them, "Don't feel shy or embarrassed when you speak English with an accent. It shows you know two languages and that is impressive."

I say this to them when they tell me how embarrassed they feel trying to use their English in public while also trying to understand native speakers. I understand this.

I realize I have lived for years as if everything I did was wrong and wondering what I actually wanted out of life. I decided I was through with second-guessing everything I did and every thought I had. I decided I could no longer keep smiling, pretending, nodding, and agreeing. My desperation to fit in has finally made me sick and tired of my inner critic. I am who I am, and this is the reality. I decide to stop judging myself. I had changed so much. Sometimes it is a small thing, a small insight that causes major changes in us. When I stopped judging the way I spoke English, I realized my part in the criticism of my worthiness; this colleague had not judged me, I had judged myself as unworthy.

In my country, I was considered easy going. I do not realize how hot bloodied I am until I observe how cool and emotionally detached most Canadians are. I no longer belong to the warm comfort of my country, nor do I feel that comfort of belonging here in my new home. It's an ache, a sharp pain that only an immigrant who has moved to a new country later in life knows. It feels like constant constraint.

I reflect on my mom's life. She experienced pain from not fitting in to her society. She was made to marry at thirteen. She was forced to stop performing and was ridiculed for her work with Pana. I suppose that we all go through some sort of pain. The only difference is that sometimes, we choose which pain we want to experience. I had decided to leave the pain I experienced living under the rules of an Islamic country but had accepted the pains I was experiencing in my new country. I decided I was through with any pain that was holding me back.

**

Chapter Nine

It is a beautiful day in June, two years after my mother's death. On TV, I watch a show where a tightrope walker, Nik Wallenda, crosses Niagara Falls on a high wire. The whole time, I am glued to my seat, holding my breath as if to keep him safe. I am in awe of his courage and determination. My jaw literally drops as he balances on that wire high above the Falls. He arrives at the Canadian side, and is safely on dry land. A journalist asks him why he did it. He responds, "To inspire people and to show that the impossible is possible. Dreams come true."

I am truly impressed. He knew what he wanted, and he worked hard to make it happen. When I was a child, I wanted to one day become a gymnast or professional dancer. Neither was an option, since I lived in an Islamic country. My choices, according to my circumstances, were to become a doctor or an engineer. Perhaps if I had grown up here, I would be an athlete or dancer. I wonder what my life would have been like, if I had not been so restricted. I light up when I watch my favorite shows, *Dancing with the Stars* and *So You Think You Can Dance*. I imagine myself doing the steps. That could have been me. Perhaps, I think, it still could be.

I enroll in salsa classes and really enjoy it. I am a fast learner and dancing comes naturally to me, like it does most Persians. We love moving our hips and our shoulders, at parties, we wait for the music to kick in to snap our fingers, get up and move with the beat. But salsa does not feel as fulfilling as I thought. I have lost the passion I once had for dancing. I wonder what my passion is. I continue to feel empty and am not as excited as I was when I moved here full of fantasies and dreams.

I wonder if our dreams diminish as we get older, if our lights fade. I feel like reality has aged me. I dismiss the thought that I may be depressed. I know what depression feels like. I learned it after my divorce and my mom's death. I am not depressed. I am disillusioned by reality and this feels more like being slapped by the remnant of my dream to emigrate to Canada where everything would be "better." It was like some kind of message proving no matter what you do, something larger is in control. You move towards your dream and get slapped back to a different low. Who are you to have it all? People that you were close to one day become strangers. Your loved ones die. Just like that. I even find the thought of losing anyone else does not bother me. I am stunned by all the hysteria that happens after the death of a celebrity. I find myself shaking my head while people go crazy with their endless posts on social media, as the piles of teddy bears and flowers grow.

People die! I want to yell. *Young people and old; whether because of an accident or some sort of cancer. They die, people, it's normal! Nothing to get all worked up about. Geesh.* As happens, I am sobbing all of a sudden and struggling to catch my breath. *They die of cancer, just like my father. Or suddenly, just like my mother.*

I allow myself to cry and wail without telling myself to be strong and tough. I allow myself to feel my losses. I cry thinking of my father and those times he begged us to stop the chemo and let him die; I cry remembering the sight of the bloated purple body that was my mother. I cry because I miss the mountains of Tehran. I cry because I want my sister. I cry because my marriage failed as I chose someone who turned out to be so different from the person that I thought he was.

I wonder why I am no longer content and grateful with my achievements. I am a skilled and treasured teacher, yet this no longer is enough to fulfill me. "I used to dream of teaching ESL here, and now that passion, one so big it would propel me out of bed early in the morning is fading away." I gulp down a glass of water to get rid of the lump forming in my throat. I reconsider depression. After all, it is defined as a lingering sadness and lack

Chapter Nine

of enjoyment in things that once brought joy. I decide I need help because this girl isn't me. This girl from a broken but loving family wants to inspire people . . . just like Nik does. And right now, she cannot get up enough energy to even inspire herself.

I turn myself over to an obsession to learn about myself and this transforms my grief into an object of study. Learning about myself reminds me who I am. I remember and internalize that I can knock a man off a horse if I want to. For the next two years, I keep searching to get clarity. I read so many books, watch many videos and TedTalks, take many courses, and go on several retreats. Throughout it all, I ask myself, "what is my passion and purpose in life? Did I leave my home, family, friends and comfort to do the same as what I was doing in Iran?" The answer is clear and strong: hell no!

As much as I've loved teaching, I see it is time for me to quit my job as I've found a new passion. I can change more lives by sharing all that I am learning. I want everyone to be able to move past grief, an act I thought was impossible a few short months before I make this big change. Making the huge step to change professions again is hard but I sign up to become a certified coach. At first, I am intimidated by my fellow coaches-in-training, all native English-speakers, many with degrees in psychology or business. But I've been in this place of comparing myself before and this time I stand firmer and challenge myself to work through my limiting belief of inadequacy. I complete my required courses, undergo the required training hours, and pass my oral and the written tests with flying colors. By the summer of 2016, I receive my International Coach Federation Professional Coach Certificate. I am excited and proud to finally become a life coach. In a way, I feel as though I am following in my mother's footsteps.

Qualifying as a coach is just the beginning. Although I have the knowledge, skills, and lived experience to help others navigate through life's challenges, I worry about how I can make this my career. Reality hits again. I realize that I need to market myself and find clients if I wish to earn an income. A web of overwhelm grows around me but doesn't stop me. I do what has always worked for me: I get help. I hire a business coach, attend more seminars, and participate in networking events. I embrace the unknown and trust the process. I no longer allow the fear of failure to stop me from moving forward. I surround myself with inspired, like-minded peers and mentors. The process transforms my life.

That summer, I travel to Italy with three of my friends to attend the wedding of our mutual friend. For three weeks, we rent a stick-shift car and roam from Rome to the winding, tiny roads of the Amalfi coast down to the south of Italy. This was another dream come true. I had my first negroni on the busy streets of Rome where the fast stick-shift car, honking horns, drivers shouting at each other over minor infractions, architecture, food, cigarette butts that plaster the sidewalks, loud Italians, and hot weather made me feel as if I was in the streets of Tehran. In Europe, life is slower, and no one appears to be in a rush. Strangers strike up conversations over little things, men check you out at any time of the day, unlike in Canada where men only check you out only at a bar or a club. Italy felt like home.

I dare to take the train to go to Florence alone to meet a guy I met online. I rode on the back of his motorcycle while he gave me a full tour of his beautiful city: from Ponte Vecchio to the Cathedral of Santa Maria Del Fiore. We had dinner and danced at the Plaza Della Signoria where I could admire the artistic beauty of the statues of David and Medusa. Magnificent! This time though, I was wise and did not repeat my errors of my singles holiday in Mexico. I did not get drunk.

Chapter Nine

When I get back to Toronto, enlivened and shaken out of my depression, I'm ready to start a new chapter in my personal and my professional life. And one night when I am looking through profiles on an online dating site, I find Matt.

Chapter Ten

"You can have it all. You just can't have it all at the same time."

~ Oprah

As I'm checking profiles, I come across a good-looking man who's smiling and leaning on a fence holding a sword. His smile reaches right to the edges of his eyes. I see the kindness behind his nerdy glasses. He is bald and could play the brother of either Vin Diesel or Telly Savalas in a movie. It is an instant "like." His profile says he is into European martial arts, that he is a scientist, and he loves reading. I send him a wink and he sends me back a message. We get on the phone and I fall for his deep voice. We meet at an Irish pub in downtown Toronto.

"I could hear high heels coming towards me. You got to the corner of the bar and I stood up. I saw how you quickly checked me out, from head to toe, and then you gave me a big, beautiful smile. I think you liked my face, but you liked my shoes more," says Matt about our first date. Matthew always reminds me of how much he loved my confidence, my red shawl, and my toned biceps and shoulders.

For the next few dates, Matt takes me to the best steak houses in the city. We go axe throwing, to a shooting range, and to the one of the most beautiful Christmas markets in Toronto amongst the beautifully lit-up display in the Distillery district. I admire how well he planned our dates.

"You are like Wonder Woman, Sara! You've jumped out of a plane, you're a go getter, heroic, and adventurous. It's difficult to surprise you—and I want to."

He is a gentleman who opens doors for me, he is confident and knows what he wants, he knows more about the history of my country than I do, and most importantly, his hobby is fighting in medieval armour and swords. I feel safe around him. I'm so tempted to cancel my trip to see my sister for the Christmas break. I want to stay here and continue getting to know him, but I resist. "You don't want to dissolve in a man. Don't make him your priority,

Chapter Ten

Sara," I think, and I remind myself of my past relationships.

We kiss each other for the first time in the gingerbread house in the Christmas market and I fly away for two weeks. He arranges for us to go snowshoeing in the country when I return. I tell him about my preparations for a three-week business trip to Nepal as we trek through beautiful trails.

"Do you think I should go?" I asked him.

"Of course, you should! This is your business! You should take it seriously."

That's all I wanted to hear. He is not clipping my wings the way my grandfather and my father clipped my mother's and the way my ex-husband did mine. He is supportive and understanding—despite the fact I know he will miss me just as I wish I could both go on this trip yet continue these adventures which are bringing us closer and closer together.

***

It is February 2017, and I am in Nepal with one of my clients. I am her life coach. I could not have imagined this in my wildest dreams. Here I am, in Nepal, on a trip paid for by my client. I am here to coach her while we practice yoga, meditation, and mindfulness. She needed to get away from Toronto to calm her mind and she brought me with her. We stayed at a yoga and meditation center for a week, and the coaching is done in the unscheduled time. Today is a coaching day. As we talk, we hike, and we stop at a small village on the top of a mountain. I spend a day teaching English to the impoverished kids in a local school for a day. While there, we visit an orphanage as we want to sponsor a child.

We knock at the door and it swings open to a reveal a small

room filled with children aged five to fifteen. From the corner, a handsome teenage boy looks up and smiles. He irons his shirt on the floor. The little ones sit on the floor, surrounding a tiny TV. They chatter and watch with excitement, as though it is their first time looking at the animated, noisy box. The small screen is blurry. If it were up to me, I would have turned it off. I am certain that this cannot be good for their eyes. However, I am aware that it is the best version of a TV that they have. The orphanage cannot afford better.

As soon as the children notice us, they run toward us. They call me "Auntie," and give me a big hug and I hug them back. I see the hope in their eyes. Sima, one of the kids, watches over the younger ones. She is perhaps sixteen and greets us with a graceful smile. Her long, black hair is captured in a thick braided ponytail. She and Arati, a sweet little girl who cannot hold back her excitement, take me to their room. It is small but cozy and tidy. Three bunk beds take up every inch of the floor. The walls are covered with children's paintings. We sit on Arati's bed and they tell me about themselves. I learn that Arati was abandoned in the woods and brought to the orphanage by strangers who had found her.

I am so spoiled, I think to myself, as I reflect on all of the years that I wasted feeling sorry for myself. I'm all by myself. I have no one, I would say during that time and it was true. But when I look in the face of this child who was left in the woods to die, everything is brought into perspective. I wish I could adopt them and bring them to Canada with me. They clearly do not have much, yet they look happy. Perhaps their definition of happiness is different from mine. I am humbled as I recognize that happiness is never about how much we have but rather, how much we give. My mission was to help my client gain inner peace. In this environment I see how true it is that serving people, whether as a lab technologist, a teacher, or a life coach brings me lots of joy and

Chapter Ten

happiness. The more I give of my time, money, attention, and love, the more fulfilled I am.

"Where do you live, Auntie Sara?" Arati asks me.

"I live in Canada. Do you know where it is?"

"No" she says with a confused look on her cute face. She grabs my hand and drags me back in the other room to a large world map that hangs on the wall. "Show me."

"Here is your country. Nepal. And here is Canada. It's very, very far from here."

Sima has followed us to the map. She asks, "So why have you travelled all this way? Are you going to climb Mount Everest?"

I reach out for her hand. I squeeze it and give it a little kiss. I say, "I'm here because I'm following my passion and my dream. That's what I want you to do, too. Believe in yourself, dear Sima, and know that everything is possible." I know this language may seem vague to her, and we've just met, I don't know her dreams. Maybe her dream is to marry a local boy and raise a family. I hope to transfer my confidence to her through our joined hands if her goals are more challenging for her than that. It is my desire that she, and other girls like her, can live in a world where she can find peace.

Yet I look around and again I consider how spoiled I am. As I started my life out of a difficult situation, I had so much more than these children. Money and family for one. These girls would need to get opportunities for education to gain control of their destinations. I thought of the differences between us. How would she get beyond the statistics that would doom her to a shortened life in poverty? What was I doing here besides being a tourist, a voyeur of her poverty? What could I really do to make a difference

— 155 —

to the lives of the Simas and Aratis of the world?

They are so trusting these little girls. If she were older, my answer would be different. I would tell her that I am not here to climb Everest, although I would love to see its beauty. I am here with my client, who is paying for me to live my dream. Perhaps I would also tell her that I moved to Canada from Iran to feel freedom and have the opportunity to be the woman I felt I was meant to be. It is all so humbling as the trip was not about these kids, but I learned so much from this visit. Going to the orphanage and teaching at the school made me reflect on my life. It made me more grateful about what I had. I continue to send money to the orphanage hoping it makes the lives of the children there better, just as that visit improved my own life. While we stayed in that tiny village, we had to carry water to shower every day. I played with those kids, we sang Nepali songs, and at nights, I danced around a fire with the local men and women. They worked hard during the day, but they knew how to enjoy life's little pleasures. They appeared to be at peace. I reflect often about how although we have everything here in Canada, it is not frequent that people are actually at peace.

I am in a place where I can continue towards peace. I yearn for the advice of my mother. I feel that I need her to tell me that I can do it. I remember her saying that "we live in tribes," and that joy comes from being part of a community that loves each other, cares about similar things, and is involved in each other's lives. I realize that what I miss most is connection with empowered women. I desire sisterhood so I search for other Persian women, like me, living in Toronto. That's when I discover the huge population of Persian women in Canada. They are beautiful, strong, educated, elegant, fun, and meet in groups at events and self-development programs. I start hosting and facilitating some myself. I love it. Plus, I can do this work in Persian. Bonus.

Chapter Ten

I love the energy of my Persian sisters. We laugh, cry, and grow together. They share secrets with me that have not been told to anyone before. They open up about their deepest fears, insecurities, and unhappiness. They are eager to break free from their chains and step into their truth. They are tired of a culture of pleasing and perfecting. They are ready to be bold and to laugh loudly and freely.

I completely understand this. They tell me that my weekly offerings are not enough. They want full weekend retreats. I create a healing weekend program, full of yoga, meditation, coaching sessions, hikes, dance, relaxation, reflection, and rejuvenation. They love it. It is their time for self-care and now I have a business.

"Sara! When is the next retreat? I need our retreats more than ever!" Shadi, a mother of two, calls me after a long day at the hospital. She has a demanding job in risk management. I love her passion for learning and bettering her life. This is something I see in my new tribe and what I deeply value about the people I serve.

As a life coach, I feel it is a responsibility that I lead by example. I start writing articles for a Persian magazine and hosting more workshops. I grow with my clients and learn more each day. I realize that I have created the life I have been dreaming of and in the midst of this, Matt and I are falling in love.

***

I'm sitting on the couch with Matthew talking about all sorts of things. We're five months in the relationship now. He is asking me all kinds of questions to learn more about me. In reply to one of them, I said: "I wouldn't marry a man who cannot have basic communication in Persian with my family and friends." I wasn't serious, but deep down I did want my husband to show interest in my language and culture. To my surprise, he picks up his phone and registers for a Farsi class at the University of Toronto. This is it. He is showing me his love through his words and actions.

Despite all he does for me, there are days that we fight. I'm a hot-blooded Persian with an extroverted personality, and he is a cool and collected Canadian with an introverted personality. I still have difficulty trusting men, and I don't want to experience another heartbreak or loss. So, I look for every opportunity or sign to prove that this relationship is not working. He, on the other hand, is patient as he tries to prove the opposite. He suggests couple therapy. I'm in awe of a man who considers therapy before getting married. He is open-minded and committed. He genuinely loves me. He makes every effort to understand me and my past wounds. It brings tears to my eyes. I love him. He is a true knight. Chivalry is not lost.

We get engaged in the most magnificent garden in the world. The gardens of Versailles on the outskirts of Paris, France. "It's the most magical palace in Europe for the most magical lady." Matthew said after he proposed to me. Although he was too nervous to get on his knee on the boat, he managed to get the ring on my finger.

Back home, we bought and renovated a house together and planted a magnolia tree in our garden. It will forever be the reminder of Daryakenar, that beautiful spot in Iran. They say home is where your heart is. My heart is in two places, but that is okay. My home is here. Despite that, I still ach for the love, warmth, fuzziness, and sense of belonging I had in Iran, the land of my birth. This dichotomy is true for most immigrants. It is one we accept.

In Iran, we often live in some form of panic mode: unaware of who is watching, when a new war would erupt, or the repercussions from any civil disruptions. I left in order to create a life without chaos. Of course, there are still challenges in my new world, that is life, but I do not give up and I am so proud of the woman I have

Chapter Ten

become. I know I am still a work in progress. And that I plan a life with a Greek Canadian man who holds me in the highest regard is the cherry on top of a beautiful life.

Chapter Eleven

"We choose our joys and sorrows long before we experience them."

~ Khalil Gibran

My cousin, Nasim, and I are heading to Gusto 101, my favourite restaurant in Toronto. I am a Torontonian and I know that a weekday is the best time to head over to Gusto's because it is not as busy as it is on the weekends. On weekends, men and women dress to impress, hoping to find a lover. Once they are tipsy, they cannot help but show their intent. I am grateful that I am no longer in that phase of my life.

It is a Tuesday evening in October. I hold the oversized door of the restaurant open for Nasim. A host guides us up the stairs to a table in the middle of the room. I had reserved it earlier. Although it was bright outside, it is dark in here. A tiny candle lights our small wooden table and I struggle to read the menu.

"I give up!" I say in Farsi. I laugh loudly and Nasim joins in. I use my cell phone flashlight to illuminate our menus and we continue giggling.

"So, tell me more about Matt? How do you know you're in love for sure?" my cousin asks. I cannot believe that she is all grown up and married. I look into her big dark eyes, magnified behind her glasses. She is inquisitive, always was. I remember her as a serious child. As a teenager, she worked hard for a scholarship in order to pursue studies here in Canada. She does not mind the cold temperatures in Winnipeg. She is determined to get the PhD that she has aspired to.

I value her opinion and I want her to love this place like I do. I am excited to be here with family. She is excited too but for a different reason: my recent engagement. My uncles thought I was crazy when I walked out on Bahador eight years ago now. They thought I had lost my mind. I imagine how they must speak about me back home, in Tehran. I know that my engagement will be a relief to them. From their perspective, it means that I am under the protection of a man again and they need not worry about me.

Chapter Eleven

"Matt is the most amazing man I've ever met." I reply. "He is different from me, less of an extrovert, but he does things that surprise me. He's very cautious and he carefully examines every decision he makes. Yet at the same time, he is very easy going. When we went to Costa Rica, he did the superman zipline with me without any hesitation. I was surprised as he hates heights and that zipline is the longest and one of the scariest ziplines in South America."

"And I hear he is learning Farsi! How amazing that he is doing that," Nasim says.

"I *love* when he speaks Farsi. I laugh—

"You laugh at him?" she interrupts.

"… because he sounds so cute! Plus, he does the same thing to me. He'll say, 'Say that again, *joonam*, say that again!' Matt begs me to repeat some words in English that he says I mispronounce. I love when he speaks Farsi and he thinks it is cute when I say certain words in English, like 'ugly,' 'stupid,' 'milk,' and 'yeah.'" I laugh and Nasim joins me.

She smiles at me and says, "I can't help laughing when you laugh! You throw your head back, and you are so full of joy. I feel your passion for life when I am with you. It makes me feel less serious and it feels so good." I tell her that having the freedom to laugh without worrying that I am laughing too loud and will be considered immoral is a relief. I laugh when I find enjoyment and the lightness of being able to laugh adds to my pleasure.

"So," Nasim asks, "when will you get married? Will the uncles come here, or will you be married in Tehran?"

"I am not sure. Matt loves to visit Iran and my family, and he probably wants to get married in Tehran more than I do. It isn't a big deal to me. We may just go, the two of us, to Toronto City Hall and just get it legally done, with no big fuss. But he says he wants to get married in Iran or in a British castle. My knight loves the history of England. He belongs to the medieval era! He wants us to get married and kneel at a statue of King Arthur. I told him that I will *not* kneel in front of him, nor anybody else, let alone a statue!" I laughed the day Matt told me of this odd desire. "'What do you want me to do next?' I had asked him. 'Call you 'milord?'"

Nasim sits back in her chair, seemingly shocked by my reply. "Getting married is no big deal?" She leans forward and peers into my eyes. "It seems you really know what you want, Sara!"

"Matt understands me. He respects me. He cares deeply about me. He's wonderful! He lets me be me, not that he could stop me." I laugh and she laughs with me. "I will never lose myself in a man again. Not ever. It is more important to have this connection with Matt than to waste money entertaining everyone for a single afternoon."

Nasim nods in approval. "You've changed, Sara." Her voice is quiet.

"I know I have changed. I worked hard to change."

The waiter comes and I switch back to English. "Two glasses of negroni, with ice." I order us a dinner of pizza and kale salad with roasted nuts, parmigiana, and lemon vinaigrette.

Nasim continues: "You always cooked Persian food. Remember? Always. Every single day! Don't tell my mom, but I always liked your *loobiya polo* more than hers."

"Are you serious? Your mom is one of the best cooks ever." I sip my negroni and smile as I remember life as a young bride.

"And I remember your hair after you got married. It was long,

Chapter Eleven

black, and thick like your mother's," she says.

I try to see myself through her eyes. I see a short-haired stylish woman in her early forties with bright red lipstick: a woman whose eyes shine bright with confidence and ambition. We do not look out of place here. We are part of Toronto's mosaic, with people of all races and religions. Toronto is considered to be the most diverse city in the world. Countless languages are probably spoken in this packed restaurant. I look around and wonder how they got here and what their stories are.

I went from playing the part of a good girl in Tehran to being what I am now. From drowning in grief and anger, to being able to think back to my former marriage with nostalgia. I am happy. I feel at peace. Nasim is right, I have changed. I sit in front of her, spending a small fortune on a meal that is a true culinary experience. And I do not need a man to pay my way.

Later, when it is time for my cousin to return to the airport, she mentions she would take the express train on her own. I don't object. I would have forced her to accept the double inconvenience of me driving her to the airport even a few years ago. That is the Persian thing to do. Instead, I wave her off, standing arm in arm with Matt as we watch her head to the train station where she'll catch the Airport Express. I think of all the choices she has in front of her. Iranians value education and both women and men with master's degrees often work as professors and other key knowledge providers in our chosen countries. I wonder what my cousin's future has in store as she obtains her PhD. Will she put her studies or career aside to have children? If she doesn't, will she be content with her choices?

I could see that Nasim, too, knew what she wanted. She did not let the expectation of being a good Iranian woman hold her back, and she was in a different time now and a different place than

I was at her age. She need not juggle and compromise as I did and as my mother did. And now I help women who are not as focused and strong as Nasim to make empowered choices, ones that are right for them. I cannot think of a better way to honor my mother and carry her legacy. Grief is forever a part of life, but I use it to fuel my purpose.

***

Sometimes it all feels so finished and perfect. Then there are days like today. Today it feels like my whole body is aching. Literally aching, but not from a workout or any physical activity but from stress and the pain of the mental work of always trying to remember the rules. Of fitting in. The pain of stretching and striving, the pain of growing and becoming somebody, the pain of proving myself. The pain of the voice, the voice that never stops reminding me that I am not truly Canadian:

Who do you think you are Sara? Why do you think you can make an impact? It takes you hours to finish your school assignments. When will you be satisfied enough to stop investing in learning? You could not even get into University of Toronto. Instead, you are doing your master's degree in an online university!

Now I hate it when people ask me where I'm doing my master's degree, just like the time before, when I taught English as a second language and cringed when asked about my job. Then I didn't want people to ask me what I did for a living because my English wasn't perfect. Now I have some shame because I am not studying at "the best" university that is just down the road from my former condo. And speaking of English, I thought I'd feel less ashamed with time and after leaving the teaching profession, but no, that hasn't been the case. I still have my moments. I'm an author and a speaker now. How on earth can I still make mistakes in my spoken English? Will there ever be a time when I do not judge myself so harshly? I

Chapter Eleven

am a professional and respected speaker in a new language, with a loving partner, a beautiful home. When will the striving stop? Perhaps, I will never know how to define "enough."

On my journey to go up the achievement and victory ladder, I push Matt too.

"What is your vision? What is your life purpose? What is your next goal?" I ask him when I see him watching Netflix. He is watching TV while I'm struggling with my schoolwork, trying to figure out how to write a research paper after twenty years away from academic life.

"I'm happy the way things are. I don't have to tie my happiness to a goal," he replies in his cool and confident voice. "Plus," he continues, "I studied and worked hard all my life. It's time for me to relax."

How can he be happy and content like that? I wonder. It's not the time to relax at all. I tell him that he can either help me with my business or he should challenge himself to do something new. "How is this going to work in the long run if we're not going at the same pace?" I say. "We'll end up growing apart like my parents!"

"Why do you keep bringing it up?" he asks. "I understand you are wounded and have past traumas. But even John Gottman says that he and his wife were so different, yet they loved each other. I feel like you want to change me and make sure we're always *exactly* on the same page. You want to make sure everything works perfect in our relationship just like the way you want to get a perfect score on your assignments!"

I can feel his confusion and frustration. I'm wounded, but I'm trying. I wish I could be as content as he is, but I have this drive in me. I am a badass go-getter. I need to prove to myself that I can achieve any goals I set and right now my goal is to make myself known in a country where I feel ten years behind. It could be that starting over again is what causes my drive to move through the process of building a business so much faster than others. I am definitely a work in progress that while seeking peace does things that perhaps push "peace" away, further out and into the future. I wonder if I'd be doing the same if I had not left Iran. I know I wouldn't be aching as much though. I wonder why I cannot work a 9-5 job and be happy like so many other people can. Isn't it enough that I made it to Canada? That I learned to live with my losses? That I have a wonderful man in my life? That I made friends?

Why do I have to write a book? Have a thriving and successful business? Go back to school? Get on stages, go viral, and have an impact?

Maybe it is some kind of "immigrant thing?" Maybe because I am making up for those years of my life that I fell behind. The years that I came here and had to get a brand-new beginner's driver's licence as if I hadn't had fifteen years of driving experience. Consider the many people who were engineers, dentists, doctors, judges in their homelands, but here they cannot continue in the fields in which they once excelled.

So, maybe it is an immigrant thing where you feel like your whole brain is aching, like some kind of brain flu. At times feels like that good soreness you get after a work-out. But still, I get swept over, as if by a sudden gust of a strong wind, with a general feeling of being unsettled mixed with a melancholic desire to feel at peace. An ache. As Oprah famously said, "You can have it all. Just not all at once."

***

I feel like I've lived two lives—the life before I emigrated and the life afterwards. The life before that wasn't at all perfect, but still,

Chapter Eleven

during that life I felt content because my loved ones were around. My dad, my mom, my grandparents, my uncles, my friends, and my ex-husband. There was love, our cottage, warmth, and even arguments but I felt that sense of belonging and togetherness.

Then I moved. I've been building everything from scratch—my identity, my friendships, my career, my network, my connections, my community. It feels like I was reborn into a new person. Brené Brown says that true belonging never asks us to change who we are. It demands that we be who we are. My mom wanted to be who she was, and I want to be who I am. My mom did it her way and I'm doing it my way.

"Sara, how do you get out of your comfort zone?" a client asked me.

I had to pause to think. "I have been out of my comfort zone since I left my country. I don't even know how it feels to live within your comfort zone anymore. I get what I compare to rashes. *Kahir mizanam*. Itchy for change. That's how I know it's time to stretch myself. I decide to pick a challenge, I get help, and I jump right into it. I'm addicted to the pain of growth."

I have done it so many times that even Matt was inspired to join me.

"Remember when we started dating what you told me about self-development?" I asked him when I saw him listening to well-known personal growth gurus and upgrading his skills for a higher position at work.

"Yes," he replied. "I said don't even think about getting me into your world. I like my comfort zone."

Yet here he is. Shifting with me.

And I have to shift to meet Matt's world. In Tehran, we blow up and cool off as nothing ever happened. That's our Middle Eastern blood. It boils fast and cools faster. My mom and I would fight one minute and kiss and make up the next second. Matt and I went through couple therapy for more than a year because what I grew up with is considered anger issues here. It's all about stretching and growth.

My mother was ahead of her time and died too young and too suddenly. Her country was not ready for her independence and free spirit. It still is not. She did what she could to grow, better understand the people around her, and do the work she loved. She made the decisions that were right for her and fought to be true to herself. She fought for a divorce as a teenager, left a husband who made her feel small and yet nursed that same man through his illness and death. She did what her conscience and soul told her to do.

Now, I do the same. I continue to learn while I support women who want to live full of authenticity. I have helped women to reach out and reach within in order to create fulfilled lives. And I support by using what I learned through my life and my mother's lives as women who both serve other women. My dear Maman had pain in her home, the place that brings me feelings of family and connection. She knew the pain of not fitting in her society: having to marry at thirteen, being forced to stop performing, being ridiculed for her work with the School of Pana. Her aches were different from mine, and mine are likely to be different to yours. We all go through some sort of pain. But the hope is we live long enough and learn and love enough to turn that pain to power—because, truly, it is up to us whether we suffer or find meaning through it. Little Sara, I may be, but my words, my courage, and my devotion make me feel giant in the face of resistance to living a true life.

Chapter Eleven

\#daretobebold

\#daretobeyou

Acknowledgements

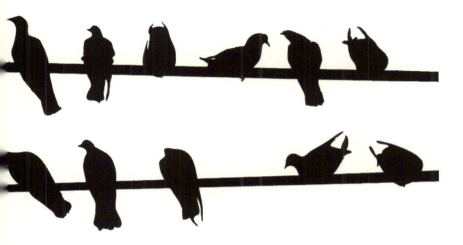

This memoir would have not been possible without the love and support of so many people.

My angels, my parents, whose memories kept me writing when I was fearful, tired, and doubtful.

Mom, I can't even finish the sentence without shedding tears. You know you were my 'why' for writing this book. You are forever my number one role model.

Dad, thank you for your unconditional love. You raised me to be an independent woman.

My sister, my partner in crime when we were teenagers. I have always admired your perseverance, drive, and strength in pursuing what you have put your mind into. Your tough love made me a stronger woman when I moved to Canada. I am forever grateful for that.

My uncles, thank you for always being a big part of my life.

Shahin, my amazing uncle. You became my biggest support after I lost my mom. You were the one who encouraged me to publish my book when I expressed my fear and hesitation. Thank you for believing in me and supporting me the way my mom did.

Matthew, my love, my rock, thank you for wiping my tears so lovingly every time I cried because I was missing my parents, I was unsure, I was scared, or I was overwhelmed. Thank you for constantly reminding me how far I have come and how strong I can finish. Thank you for giving me the freedom to be who I want. Your presence in my life has been the best thing that happened to me after all the loss and pain I went through.

Jackie Brown, words cannot express my gratitude for you. You patiently listened to my story and skillfully developed it. You learned about my culture, laughed at some craziness, and cried with me. You've been on this journey with me for more than 3 years! There were times that we got frustrated, we drove each other crazy, we took a break, but we did NOT give up! You always said: "Sara! You have a beautiful story to tell. We are almost done. You can do this!" And we did! Thank you for your love, understanding and endless support. You are now officially half Persian.

Tabitha, my publisher, I first fell in love with your passion, beautiful soul and your smile. Thank you for reading the manuscript so carefully and giving opinions so compassionately. Thank you for being so patient and understanding when I was too tired to make any changes. You said: "I want you to fall in love with your story Sara." And I did. You and your team worked tirelessly to bring my dream book cover into reality. I'm truly grateful for

Acknowledgements

your love and support.

To Shahab Anari, my business coach, thank you for giving me the confidence to grow.

To my dear friends, Azadeh, Hadis, Negin, and Sharareh, we may be million miles away from each other, but you have been my biggest cheerleader squad.

To all other friends, coaches, classmates, followers, and clients who either inspired me or cheered me along the way, Thank you! You all have a special place in my heart.

And to all people who helped little Sara become who she is today.

About the Author

About the Author

Sara is a Professional certified life coach, a member of the International Coach Federation, a best-selling co-author, a member of the Canadian Association of Professional Speakers (CAPS) and a Grief Recovery Specialist. She has been featured on Rogers TV, and in Shahrvand, IranStar and Tehranto Magazine. She's currently pursuing her master's degree in counselling psychology where she can combine her life experiences with scientific research to help people face their fears, rediscover their authentic self and overcome life challenges. Sara believes it takes courage to be you, to be true to yourself and to live a life you love!

Little Sara of Tehran

Manufactured by Amazon.ca
Bolton, ON